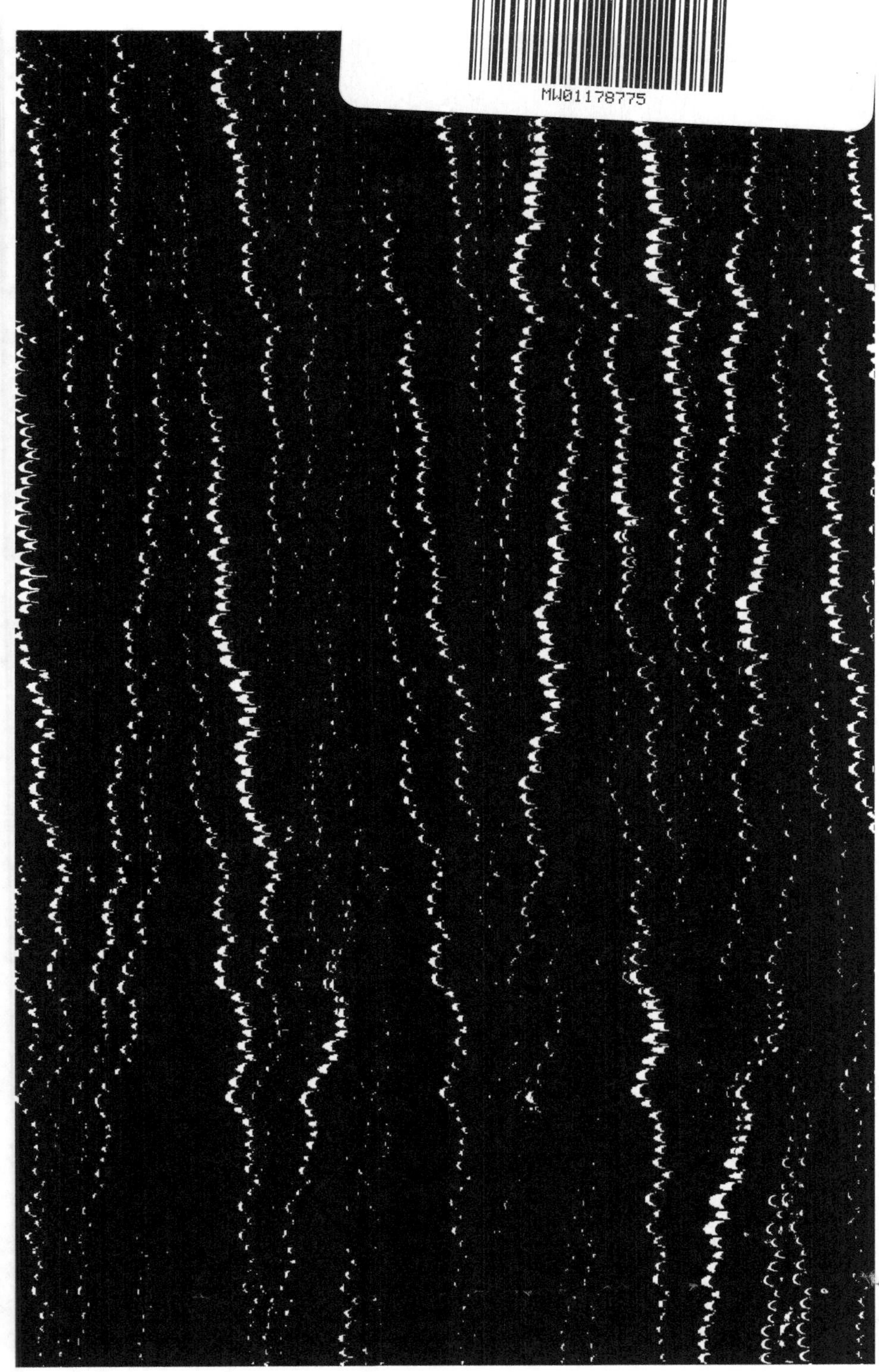

INJURIOUS INSECTS

OF

MICHIGAN.

By A. J. COOK,

OF THE MICHIGAN STATE AGRICULTURAL COLLEGE.

INSECTS INJURIOUS TO THE FARM, GARDEN, AND ORCHARD.

BY PROF. A. J. COOK OF THE STATE AGRICULTURAL COLLEGE.

PREFACE.

The following report is arranged with the express desire that it may become a practical hand-book to every husbandman in our State. It is intended solely as an insect manual to the farmer, gardener, and fruit-grower, which shall give all possible information as to the best means to ward off insect enemies, and will be pruned of all scientific terms and technicalities not absolutely needed for the accomplishment of the desired end. It is greatly hoped that in spreading this information broadcast over our State, *all* our tillers may be stimulated to practice the measures recommended, for without concerted action to the fullest extent, this important problem of insect injuries can never be perfectly solved. Will not every farmer into whose hands it may fall, every grange, club, and society, horticultural and agricultural, if only for selfish ends, see that every farmer in the vicinity procure it, and then all work together to make it in the largest degree useful?

Those insects which attack our field crops are first considered, next the insect pests of our gardens, and lastly, the enemies of our orchards and vineyards. In each division the insects are considered somewhat in the order of their importance.

The scientific name of each insect will be placed in a parenthesis, and can be passed over when desired.

In the preparation of this manual, free use has beem made of the valuable reports of Messrs. Riley, Fitch, Le Baron, and Walsh; the American Entomologist, Practical Entomologist, and the important works of Harris, Curtiss, and Packard.

The illustrations are from drawings made by Prof. Riley, and so need no praise.

COLORADO POTATO BEETLE.

Doryphora 10-lineata—Say. Sub-Order *Coleoptera*. Family *Chrysomelidæ*.

If any one should doubt that this late comer among our pests takes first rank as an enemy to our field crops, he would only need to glance at the market columns of any of our journals to become speedily convinced of his error. What signifies the fact that potatoes are quoted, and have been for the past two or three years, even in the rural journals, at one dollar and upwards per bushel, unless it means that the potato beetle is fast converting a common article of diet into a luxury? Nay, more, it asserts that even known remedies are slow of application. Though in this case we have a very cheap and perfectly effective remedy, still, actual observation and the high price of potatoes prove that barely half our farmers make use of it. There can be no doubt that should this article induce all our farmers "to fight the potato beetle by the most approved method," it would add at least $100,000 to the wealth of our State the coming year.

HISTORY.

The history of this beetle, that it is a native of Colorado, where it was discovered, named, and described by Say, many years ago; how, on a bridge of potato vines, it invested our western States less than a score of years since, and from thence spread rapidly eastward till it now has actually gained our Atlantic coast, where it only awaits opportunity to take passage for Europe, where it will continue its dreaded ravages in the green fields of the Emerald Isle,—all this is already well known.

NATURAL HISTORY.

The natural history of the potato beetle is also familiar to most of our farmers. It comes forth out of the earth as a beetle just as the potato vines are peering from the ground. Sometimes, as the creature stands over the hill, it seems fairly to grin in expectant longing for the rich, tender feast which nature is about to spread. With the coming of warm days the female (Fig. 1, *d*) lays her clusters of orange eggs (Fig. 1, *a*), sometimes to the number of a thousand,—a single beetle which I confined laid over eleven hundred eggs,—either on the under side of the leaves of the potato vines, or on blades of grass or other vegetables near by.

Fig. 1.

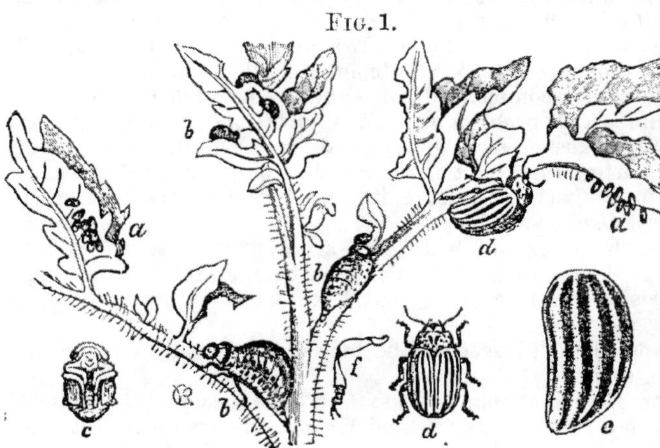

a eggs; *b* larva; *c* pupa; *d* imago; *e* wing-cover, magnified; *f* leg.

These soon hatch, when the young or larvæ (Fig. 1, *b*) are found to eat quite as voraciously as the mature beetle. In about fifteen days the young become fully developed, when they pass into the ground to pupate (Fig. 1, *c*). After about ten days of such quiet they come forth in the beetle state, and from their freshness it might be thought that the old-time beetles had been absent to get a new suit, and had just returned to show their finery.

These beetles, with their bright bands of yellow and black, mate, deposit eggs, and soon die, behaving in all respects as before. So, too, the larvæ and pupæ. These again are followed by a third brood, which completes the ruinous work of the season: but the pupæ of this last brood do not come forth in ten days, nor do they die; but, resting quietly beneath the earth, seem to be gathering strength for a miserable repetition of the previous year's abomination.

WILL THEY REMAIN WITH US?

It is hoped by many that these incorrigible pests will not be long among us, reasoning from analogy, as many insects (like the Hessian fly) have been quite as destructive for a time, and then have almost entirely vanished. We may reasonably hope that the insect enemies of this beetle, which are rapidly increasing, will lessen its numbers yearly; but that we shall ever be rid of it is reckoning without our host. It will probably remain with us for all time, though as its natural enemies become more numerous they will doubtless hold it in check so that some years the evil will be very slight. Still it is safe to conclude that we shall have to be ever ready to give it battle, and well may we be grateful that such efficient weapons are at our command.

REMEDIES.

Inasmuch as Paris green is so practical, so efficient, and so cheap a remedy for this pest, I shall, in this place, do what every farmer had better do on his farm,—ignore all other means, such as hand picking, machinery, etc., as too expensive, and not sufficiently thorough. With a little care, Paris green,—the genuine article, of course,—is entirely safe, and we may well welcome the change of its use from our beautiful green-tinted wall-papers, where its poisonous exhalations have long gendered disease and death, to the richer green of our potato-fields.

The two methods which have been tried at the college with the best success as to economy, are either to mix the green with water, a heaping tablespoonful to ten quarts of the fluid, and sprinkle on with a common sprinkler or an old broom; or to mix the green with flour in the proportion of one part of green to six of flour, sifted on when there is no dew on the vines, either through a muslin bag suspended to a convenient handle, that it may be carried and shaken over the vines, the person making the application walking upright, or with a pail, the bottom being of fine wire gauze or finely perforated tin. Where these methods are used, the whole expense per acre, for both material and cost of application, will not exceed five dollars for the season.

The advantages of the water mixture are ease, safety, even with the careless, and rapidity of application, and that too, even if the day is windy. Its disadvantages are waste of material, as nearly one-third of the water does not touch the vines, and of course is lost; danger of not stirring the mixture sufficiently often, when the green, being only held in suspension, not dissolved, settles to the bottom, and the preparation becomes too dilute; ease with which the green when thus applied is washed off by heavy rains; and the danger of not applying evenly, as the powder suspended in the water is amassed wherever the drops of water settle. Yet from its convenience, and the ease with which the application may be made, this will quite likely be the favorite method.

After careful experimenting, I have found the flour mixture preferable to all other preparations. The flour makes the green adhere to the vines so that the heaviest rain is powerless to remove it. No second application is needed till enlarged growth of vines demands it. I make the mixture strong,—one of powder to six of flour,—so that in making the application we need add only just enough of the mixture that we may be able to see it on the vines. The danger of using the flour mixture consists in the fact that unless used sparingly, the paste will destroy the vines. But it is perfectly easy and entirely safe to use it if the least possible amount be used. I repeat, add only enough that it may be seen.

I have thus been enabled to safely apply this mixture even to our tender melon and cucumber vines. I would not apply it when the dew is on, as the application will be more even if the vines are dry, and with the strength recommended above will always prove effectual. I think this is the most economical method yet recommended. By using the flour mixture I have found that two applications are always sufficient for our early varieties, and frequently for later ones; and three applications are in any case all that are needed, even in seasons of heaviest rains. Some prefer to use plaster instead of flour, using forty or fifty parts of plaster by measure to one of the green. This does not form a paste, and can be added in quantity without danger to the vines,—indeed the plaster may be useful,—but the first heavy rain will wash it off.

ENEMIES.

I might enumerate and describe the score or more of natural enemies, birds and insects, which attack and destroy this potato beetle; but as they will not for long years, if ever, make the use of Paris green unnecessary, and as this article is only to deal with practical problems, I will omit this interesting part of the subject. Now, will not all who read this article

PRACTICE THIS REMEDY,

and thus make a blessing out of a curse? For if, by expending $5 per acre, we can save our crop, and get, as is true all over the State, fifty cents more per bushel than in ante-beetle days, we shall surely sustain the paradox of being indebted to a sore enemy for an increased profit of $40 per acre on our potato crop. How pertinent the following from H. Vorhees of Ottawa county, in the New York Tribune:

"I see now how I might have made much money; for the price of potatoes has doubled. I find the cost of applying Paris green is not more than $5 an acre, and it is a sure remedy. Yet there are those right here who spend fifty days' labor, hand-picking, per acre."

Is not the Detroit Tribune quite right in saying that no one has any moral right to neglect insect pests and thus bring evil to others? With slight care this remedy is entirely safe. Of course no one need eat or breathe the poison, while the danger of poisoning the earth, lately heralded forth by that first scientific entomologist of our country, Dr. J. L. Le Conte, was shown by Professor Kedzie of our own college, some years since, to be entirely groundless. It is strange that so able and careful a scientist as Dr. Le Conte should lend his great name in fostering such expensive errors.

CUT-WORMS.

Agrotians. Family, *Noctuidæ.* Sub-Order, *Lepidoptera.*

Little, if any, inferior to the potato beetle in its destruction to our field crops, is the cut-worm. The cut-worms (for there are several species which claim tribute from the grain-grower), are not confined in their operations to a single staple, for nearly all our cereals, grasses, and especially our corn crops, are made to contribute to their support.

The cut-worms are so named from their prodigal habits of cutting off plants;

not taking their fill on a single plant, leaving all uneaten undisturbed, but, as if totally depraved, rejoicing in rioting and wantonness, they simply cut the plants asunder, thus ruining every plant that they attack.

These destroyers are called surface caterpillars in England, doubtless from the fact that they lie concealed by day just beneath the earth surface. In Europe they are dreaded from their effect on grasses, and such injury in this country, though less patent than that done to corn, is by no means inconsiderable. In Europe the loss of a third of a crop is ruinous; here it is common, and hardly causes comment.

The cut-worms are no foreigners, "being to the manor born." Even the Indians found in them a foe fully as persistent if not as formidable as the white man.

NATURAL HISTORY.

The natural history of these insects (and this will apply to those which ravage our gardens and orchards as well as those attacking field crops), is as follows: Some time, usually late in the season, the moths, which are always of a sober hue, gray or brown, with two conspicuous spots on their front wings, may be seen in concealed places about our houses, as being attracted by lights they come into our houses by night, and being night moths, seek to hide by day.

FIG. 2.

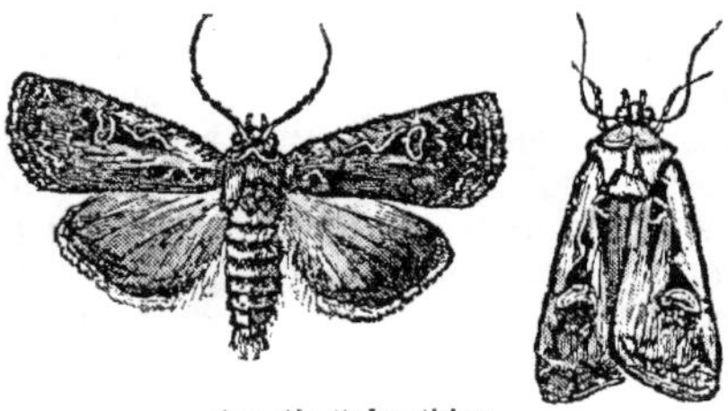

Agrotis Subgothica.

It is probable that the moths, after pairing, seek some grass spot on which to deposit eggs, for true it is that we find the caterpillars, in fall and spring, amidst the roots of grass on which they appear to feed, though even these immature larvæ may, like the mature ones, come forth for the more succulent blade and leaf. And among all insects there is a strange instinct which seldom errs, which secures egg-laying in close proximity to the food of the larvæ. In sooth, there are some flies which only sip the liquid sweets of flowers, yet seem to remember their former less refined diet, as they place their eggs in the midst of carrion filth or stable refuse, on which their maggot progeny seem to feed with unfailing relish.

The young cut-worms, perhaps from their small size and abundant food, seem to attract little attention because of their injuries till the succeeding May, when the full grown larvæ, now over an inch in length, greasy, and in sober garb of gray, brown, or striped with light and dark, depending on the species, come forth to nip our crops and blast our hopes.

FIG. 3.

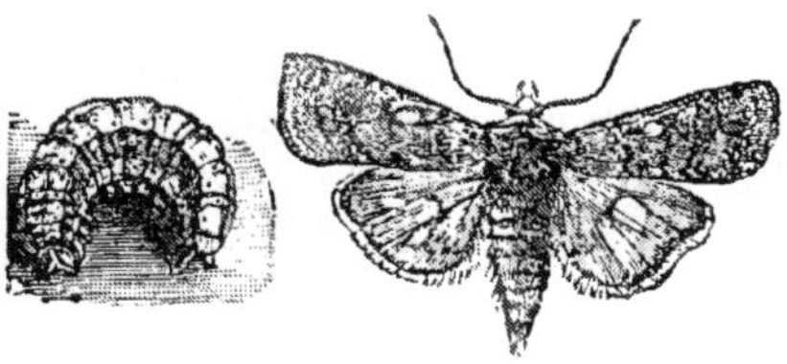

Agrotis Cochrani,--Larva and Imago.

After the larvæ growth is complete they become chrysalids in an earthen cocoon, a few inches from the surface, and in summer and autumn the moths again appear, when the same cycle of growth, changes, and destruction is again repeated.

FIG. 4.

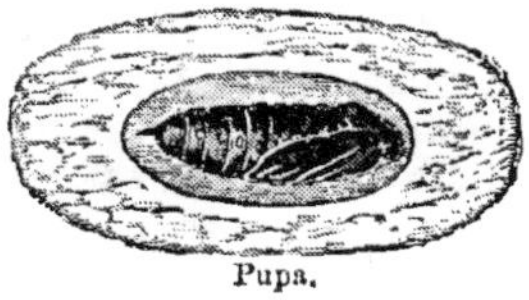

Pupa.

I might describe here, as before, many predaceous and parasitic insects which help to hold these dread destroyers in check, but as they are unable, without aid, to wholly accomplish the good work, I will at once proceed to the more practical duty of detailing artificial means to preclude these injuries.

REMEDIES.

I am fully persuaded that there is no more sure way to ward off cut-worm injuries than to enter into partnership with the birds, in which it shall be the duty of the party of the first part to plow the land early in the fall, so that bluebird, robin, and grakle may have a cut-worm feast before leaving for more genial climes. Deep harrowing will aid the party of the second part, while a repetition of the same as early in the spring as the season will permit, will insure a thanksgiving repast of the same nature. I feel very certain that from this cause, and not freezing of the larvæ, has originated the unquestionable fact that fall plowing is an advantage. When unprotected larvæ can survive a temperature –30°, as I have proved the past winter, we may be slow to credit the freezing method of destruction.

Our early spring birds are much put to it to gain sufficient food for themselves and brood, and with the opportunity will become chief abettors in cut-worm destruction. That the three birds above named do merit loudest praise for such valuable service I have personal proof.

The only method to supplement the above measures when they are not adequate to remove the evil, with our field crops, is digging out by hand and destroying. This is by no means so tedious a procedure as would be thought at first, as by passing along the corn-field early in the morning the cut stock will reveal the whereabouts of the night-marauder, which, by digging around the stub, may soon be found and crushed. As this plan implies the loss of at least a single stock to a larvæ, it would be very well in planting to practice the advice of the poet: "Two for the blackbird, two for the crow (they have earned them), two for the cut-worm, and four to grow." This advice will be all the more pertinent if the corn is to be planted after late spring-plowed greensward; I need hardly say late, as our wet springs usually necessitate late spring plowing.

If our farmers will heed the above, and give the go-by to all those quack remedies which obtain annually an unmerited place in our periodicals, such as salt, plaster, etc. (though all fertilizers which promote rapid growth are always to be commended as aids in the work of insect destruction), this cut-worm evil will soon assume less importance.

The following are the species which I have found injurious to our corn crops in this State: *Agrotis nigricans*, Linn.; *Agrotis devastator*, Brace; *Agrotis subgothica* (see Fig. 2d), Howorth; and *Hadena amputatrix*, Fitch. These species are all on exhibition in the college museum, and those desiring full descriptions of them in all stages will find them all in Riley's and Fitch's reports.

THE MAY BEETLE.

Lachnosterna fusca, Frohl. Family, *Scarabeidæ*. Sub-Order, *Coleoptera*.

Few farmers will need a description of that sleek old culprit, the white grub, —still less to be assured of its destructive powers, as the damage to our meadows and other products are becoming yearly more alarming. If I mistake not, this is considered in some portions of our State, especially the southwest portion, the farmer's worst insect pest.

NATURAL HISTORY.

I need hardly say that in May and June the beetles (3 and 4, Fig. 5), all brown and plump, come forth from the ground, and at early twilight, and on into the night, fly forth in such numbers as to sound like the swarming of bees, often annoying us by thumping at our windows or lumbering into our rooms, to be felled by bumping the walls; hence the name dor-beetle, and the expressions "beetle-headed," and "blind as a beetle." These beetles often do no inconsiderable damage by eating the foliage from our fruit trees, though here at the college they have seemed to prefer the oak leaves. Would that they might rest content with the completion of such mischief. After pairing, the females lay their eggs, fifty or more, probably in the ground, near the roots of grass or other plants.

FIG. 5.

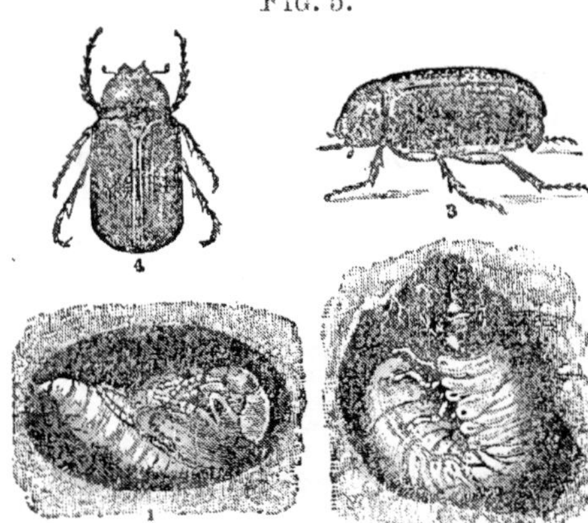

1, pupa; 2, larva; 3 and 4, imagoes.

The grub, white, wrinkled, with a brown head (2, Fig. 5), feeds on the roots of grass, wheat, corn, and other plants for three years, when it becomes full-grown, having attained nearly one and one-half inches in length. In the third autumn it forms a cocoon of earth, in which it pupates (1, Fig. 5). The next May or June the beetles come forth to enjoy a brief riot, and prepare for another round of mischief under ground.

REMEDIES.

As the number of these beetles and grubs are frequently so alarmingly great, and their mischief so wide spread and extensive, we can only hope to ward off their ravages in our pastures and meadows by wholesale remedies. So soon as the meadow turns sear, and we have the further evidence that the white grub is the culprit in the grass, now rootless, freely yielding to the hand or rake; or, still better, finding the sleek old gormand beneath by a little digging; if this state of things is so extensive as to create uneasiness, the field better be given over at once to the swine, and the more swine the better. It may be as profitable to turn the grass into pork, indirectly through the aid of the white grub, as to change it directly into beef or mutton; besides, we then are sure to destroy a grievous pest. If a meadow is the seat of the evil, it may pay best to cut the hay first. Early fall plowing will enable the birds to aid the swine, and possibly kill the grubs by destroying their food. Frequent harrowing will give the birds a still better chance to indulge in this "feast of fat things."

In protecting our wheat and corn, the same remedies would apply as those recommended to destroy the cut-worm.

As yet, we know no method to fight these pests of our meadows, except the one given above; and if the ravages appear while the grub is in the first or second year's operation, which can be ascertained by the size, the above method of procedure will be still more desirable.

THE WHEAT MIDGE.

Cecidomyia tritici, Kirb. Family, *Cecidomyidæ*. Sub-Order, *Diptera*.

Unlike its near relative the Hessian fly (*Cecidomyia destructor*), the midge or wheat berry fly, is not yet driven from among us, though *its* many insect enemies have so depleted its numbers, that it no longer fills our agriculturists with dark forebodings as to the future of our wheat interests.

NATURAL HISTORY.

The natural history of the midge is as follows: The little orange fly, so small as to almost escape notice, appears in June. The eggs are laid on the chaff of the berry. Upon hatching, the orange-colored maggot lies between the chaff and berry, and by absorbing the juices, ruins the kernel, and thus an insignificant larval fly does immense damage.

REMEDIES.

This imported enemy, which does no great damage in Europe, because of the numerous parasites which prey upon it, is fast losing its terrors here, and so I will only mention the very commonly understood preventives:

If they are troublesome, get the variety of grain which is least affected, and then sow fall wheat so early, and spring wheat so late, that the former may mature too early to be injured, the latter, too late.

WIRE-WORM.

Elater. Family, *Elateridæ*. Sub-Order, *Coleoptera*.

Within a few years, these insects have become quite destructive in our State. Complaints have came to me from all points, in reference to injuries done to corn and potatoes.

NATURAL HISTORY.

FIG. 6.

Wire-worms, the larvæ of elater, or spring-beetles, usually feed on rotten wood, so that we can hardly raise a piece of bark on a decaying log, or turn over a rotten log, without finding them. Would that all were content with such a diet; but not so, for, as too many know by disheartening experience, some of them attack the newly planted potatoes in a perfectly ruinous manner, so that to have a crop demands a second planting. Nor do they behave better towards the fresh corn plants. These wire-worms are well named, as they much resemble in form both a worm and a wire. They have the six usual jointed legs, and thus may be easily told from the myriapods, which they somewhat resemble, but which have many legs. They work for several years and pupate in an earthen cocoon. The beetles (Fig. 7) which come from these grubs, are the well-known elaters, or spring beetles, which possess such a power of springing up, if, perchance, they fall on their back. This habit, no less than their peculiar form, will serve to distinguish them wherever seen. I am not able to state what species are injurious when in the larvæ state.

FIG. 7.

REMEDIES.

The same course as that recommended for cut-worms and the white-grub,—fall plowing and frequent harrowing, to give the fall and spring birds a good chance, will also serve here. In England, where they are greatly troubled with these same or similar insects, it is common to bury potatoes with a long stick stuck through them to mark their whereabouts. This is done early,—some time before planting. The grubs collect on these to feed, when they are gathered and destroyed. Gas-lime and salt are also highly recommended by experienced gardeners of Europe. These are placed with the seed in planting.

PEA WEEVIL.

Bruchus pisi, Linn. Family, *Bruchidæ*. Sub-Order, *Coleoptera*.

This little insect, though doing little damage to garden peas, for in green peas it is not only too small to essentially change the flavor, but even to attract the eye, but in field crops, where peas are raised to feed after they are fully matured, there is very serious injury, for this little weevil, so generally distributed, and so persistent in its yearly attacks, consumes, while yet a larva, all the nutritious material of the pea; leaving only the germ and a mere shell outside. Hence, affected peas will grow, but, of course, with bated vigor; as the needed starch pabulum is wanting in those early days, the precarious time with all life; but to feed, they are almost entirely useless.

NATURAL HISTORY.

The little brown weevil, with the wing-covers so short that some light markings, somewhat resembling a letter T, are seen just back of them (Fig. 7.—*Bruchus pisi*, Linn.), comes through the winter in the peas, having a little opening (Fig. 7, *b*), a door of exit, already prepared, where they not infrequently remain even to the day of sowing. I have seen them thick as bees above the ground where peas were being sowed. Just as soon as the pods are formed and the seeds set within them, the weevil, big with eggs, if not with mischievous intent, pierces the pod opposite each pea, and inserts an egg within each puncture, so that every pea may contain within the seed of its own destruction. The larvæ, which soon hatch from these eggs, though grubs, being the young of beetles, are legless, and hence resemble maggots,—the larvæ of two-winged flies, which name is frequently applied to them. These larvæ find the young tender peas rich feeding, and by the time the peas are large enough for table use, are sleek and plump, and can easily be seen with the naked eye; and with a glass, their good feeding qualities are quickly discerned, as their tender skins seem ready to burst. By the time the peas are hard, having already eaten a hole through the shell (Fig. 7, *b*.), thus showing a foresight not rare among insects, they assume the pupa state, and change to imagoes before the time for sowing or planting the next spring.

Fig. 7.

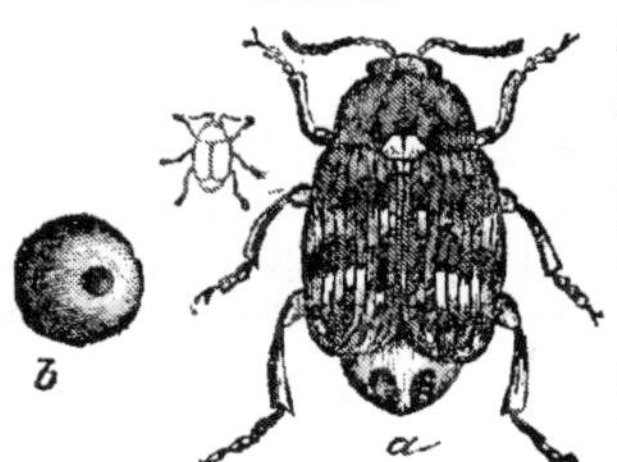

a imago magnified; *b* pea; *c* natural size.

REMEDIES.

As these insects are in the peas in the winter and in the spring, if the same be kept over one year, in perfectly close barrels, bags, cans, or bottles, of course the insects thus confined will all die. Hence, if these pea weevils are sufficiently annoying to cause disturbance, there can be a most effectual estoppel put upon their mischief by thus putting all our peas in close vessels, any time in the winter, and keeping them thus close for one season. If all would do this,—and we must have concerted action in this insect warfare,—we should soon be rid of this enemy. But the evil will be mitigated if we practice the above simply as individuals; for if the insects do find their way to our fields from those of our careless neighbors, they will doubtless come in far less numbers, and those that do come will very likely be too late to do damage, while we *may* escape entirely.

THE SQUASH BUG.

Coreus tristis, De Geer. Family, *Coreidæ*. Sub-Order, *Hemiptera*.

This old-time enemy is so well known that the figure is all that is necessary to bring his image and evil doings to mind.

NATURAL HISTORY.

The squash-bug, in common with all bugs, passes through partial or incomplete transformations, by which we mean that they are quite alike at all stages of growth, so that usually, at any stage of growth, the species would be recognized by even the unskilled in entomology. The larva, unlke the caterpillar, the grub, the maggot, is so like the imago that the relation of child and parent is easily recognized. The mature insect (Fig. 8) hibernates during winter, but by the time the melon, squash, or pumpkin vines are well up, their dusky forms, ochre yellow beneath, may be seen feeding on the leaves by day, and hid under some chip, clod, or in some crevice, by night. Soon the brown eggs are laid in clusters glued to the under side of the leaves, and the greenish larvæ, which soon become grayish, which hatch from these, commence a thorough work of despoilation, in which they are aided by their parents, which seem unwilling to die with so much good provision at hand. After a time, stubs of wings appear, which, with increased growth, is all that serves to distinguish these pupæ from their former larval condition. Nor can these afford time for quiet, like most pupæ. On the other hand, they continue to gorge themselves with the juices which they suck from the plant. Soon, they attain full growth, and fully developed wings, and are called imagos. These imagos live through the winter and are ready to repeat the same ruinous work another season.

FIG. 8.

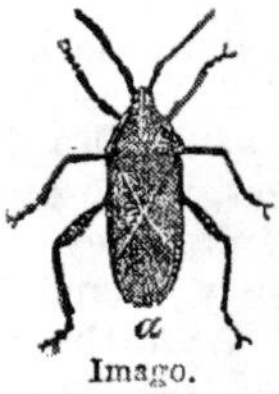

a

Imago.

REMEDIES.

The habit that these squash bugs have of concealment suggests a very practical means to capture them, which was tried here at the college the past season with perfect success. It is similar to the Ransom process for capturing the plum curculio, and consists simply in placing small pieces, boards, chips, or even green leaves on the ground, close around the vines. The bugs appropriate these as hiding places during the night. We may then go around each morning, early in the season, before the eggs are laid, and gather and destroy the bugs thus concealed, and soon extirpate the cause of the evil. These morning visits must be so early that the insects will not have yet left their hiding places. If the eggs are laid before we capture the bugs, we should either gather the eggs from beneath the leaves, or continue the same process narrated above to get rid of the young.

In all cases where mature insects come forth in the spring, of course in limited numbers, as with the potato beetle, the squash bug, etc., we shall save very much by early battle; and if we can persuade our neighbors to engage with us, the late battles and the battles of succeeding years will be but skirmishes.

SQUASH VINE ROOT BORER.

Melittia cucurbitæ, Harr. Family, *Ægeridæ*. Sub-Order, *Lepidoptera*.

This insect, a near relative of the peach-tree borer and currant borer, so troublesome along the peach belt, is becoming an evil of considerable magnitude in many parts of our State. It is no new enemy, having worked in Massachusetts and other States east for many years.

NATURAL HISTORY.

The moth, which is a beautiful orange, with deep blue wings, in common with all of this family, flies during the hottest sunshine, and with great swiftness. She lays her eggs during July and August, on the vine, close to the ground. The larva, which would be known as a caterpillar from its possessing sixteen legs, bores the base of the stem and roots, and thus entirely destroys the vines. They pupate in a rough cocoon of earth, about the roots. Dr. Packard has noticed their forming their cocoon in the stem. These are formed in autumn. The imago comes forth the next summer to inaugurate the same round of ruin.

FIG. 9.

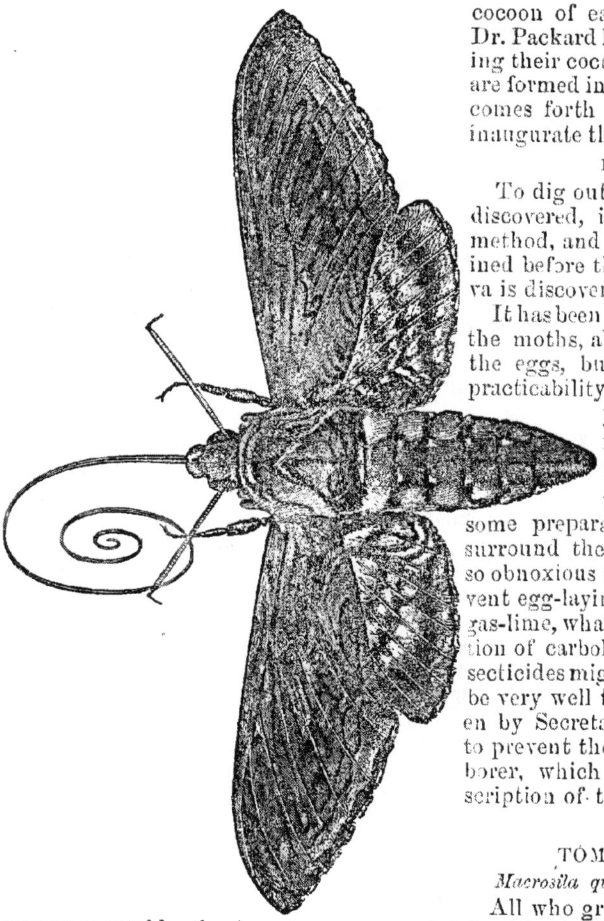

REMEDIES.

To dig out the borers so soon as discovered, is a sure but tedious method, and the vines are often ruined before the presence of the larva is discovered.

It has been recommended to catch the moths, also to carefully gather the eggs, but I much doubt the practicability of these methods, especially the latter. It is possible, and certainly very desirable, that we might discover some preparation with which to surround the vine, that would be so obnoxious to the moth as to prevent egg-laying. Limited trials of gas-lime, whale-oil soap, weak solution of carbolic acid, and other insecticides might be made. It would be very well to try the remedy given by Secretary Boteham of Ohio to prevent the work of the peach-borer, which is given in the description of that pest.

TOMATO WORM.

Macrosila quinquemaculata, Haw.

All who grow that beautiful and savory vegetable, the tomato, are acquainted with the formidable pest which, unless prevented, too often bring all our hopes of satisfied tomato appetites to naught. Who has not seen the beautiful larva, so fat and gay in its robes of deepest green, trimmed with yellow or white and beaded with the same, and who has not heard of the utterly groundless stories of its fatal horn, whose poisonous thrust it is said brings pain and death?

NATURAL HISTORY.

In July, the beautiful large gray moths (Fig. 9) appear, lay their eggs on the leaves of the tomato, not refusing potato vines in the absence of tomato plants, which they evidently prefer, at which work they may be seen early in the evening. I have frequently caught these so-called humming-bird moths around the tomato plants, or poised above flowers, where, with their long sucking-tube, they seem engaged in extracting nectar.

Fig. 10.

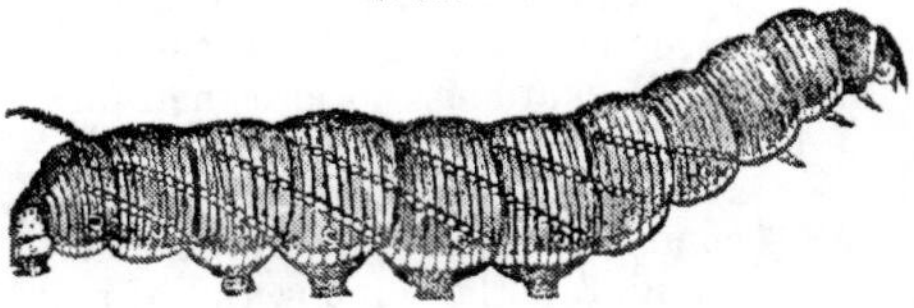

The greenish larvæ (Fig. 10) though they are not infrequently dark brown, eat voraciously, grow rapidly, and by the last of August they have not only stripped the plants of their foliage, but have become full grown, when they measure three inches in length.

Fig. 11.

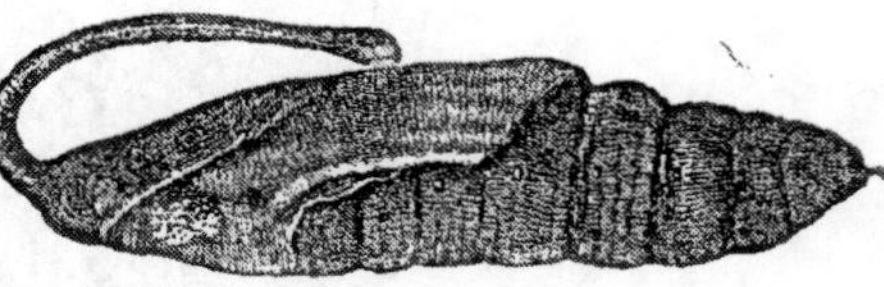

They then go into the earth, where they pupate in an earthen cocoon. The peculiar form of the pupa is a marked character of this family (Fig. 11). These brown pupæ may be found in the earth, a few inches beneath the surface, until the following summer, when the fine moth again comes forth.

REMEDIES.

Hand-picking is a quick, easy, and sure preventive. The only objection to this, so for as I know, is that it is disagreeable, and sometimes prevented by timidity. Yet I presume that a good pair of gloves will insure the temerity necessary to its successful practice. As before intimated, the fear is entirely groundless, for there are no more harmless creatures in existence. To be sure they can give quite a sharp pinch with their strong jaws, which they will attempt to do if held, and which I have often experienced while fondling them, but this is almost painless and entirely harmless. They never use their caudal horn, the supposed weapon of immemorial dread. So hand-picking, with or without gloves is entirely safe, and as effectual as safe. Of course the disfigured leaves will guide us in our search.

I have found that skunks are powerful aids in this fight, as they feed extensively on the pupæ.

CABBAGE CUT-WORMS.

Agrotis devastator, Harr.

As a full account of the natural history of the Agrotians has already been given in connection with field crops (see page 109), we need say but little of the species which is often so ruinous to our cabbage and tomato plants.

As will be remembered, the larvæ generally lie concealed by day just beneath the soil, and come forth, cloaked in darkness, to do their evil work. This is not strictly true, as frequently, on cloudy days, their eager appetites, or else an innate longing for destruction (for these cut-worms do seem the most totally depraved of all insects), impel them forth to work havoc. I have known sixty tomato plants cut off between the hours of 3 and 6 P. M.

Sandy gardens, and those near meadows, pastures, or lawns, where the insects have commenced and nearly completed their growth by feeding on the grass or its roots, are by far the most liable to attack.

REMEDIES.

After the ground is well fitted for the plants, great advantage will result from placing newly mown grass, fresh cornstalks, etc., in heaps about the plat. Coming to these by night, the larvæ will feed and crawl beneath, and may be captured and destroyed each morning. I have known large numbers to be thus entrapped. Securing those immediately within the ground to be planted, however, is not alone sufficient. These larvæ have not sixteen legs for nothing, and especially is there danger from immigrants if grass is grown contiguous to the ground planted. It might be well to continue, in such a case, to place the bunches of grass around the border of the planted area, to still attract these night marauders.

Sized paper, such as we usually write on, wound closely about the plants, and held in place by banking slightly about the base with earth, is a sure preventive, as the larvæ can not pass up its smooth surface. I have known this to be practiced with the happiest results. Care is only necessary that the paper may closely encircle the plant, and that the banking be so efficient as to surely hold it in place.

Hand-work, digging out the larvæ, is always to be commended. No more injury need be expected from these troublesome "worms," if they are once in the grasp of an irate gardener, who is disgusted at seeing his plants prostrate upon the earth. And it must give rare satisfaction to dig the culprits out from beneath the plants which their rapacity has simply cut asunder and left to wilt, and aggravate the owner, who had already reckoned up and planned to expend the proceeds from the same mutilated plants.

Here, too, especially on light soils, it will be wise to set a superfluous number of plants.

CABBAGE LEAF-ROLLER.

Plutella cruciferarum. Family, *Tortricidæ.* Sub-Order, *Lepidoptera.*

While treating of cabbage insects, I might describe the cabbage leaf-roller, or Cabbage tineid (*Plutella cruciferarum*), which little green "worms," or more properly caterpillars, mine the cabbage leaves quite disastrously, and which gray moths, with a white stripe along the back, are quite too small to produce alarm, and yet are the parents of the same green larvæ. But I will only say that I have never been troubled with them, nor have I seen much of their work. If they are annoying, it would be well to try plaster with a little turpentine mixed in, whale-oil soap solution, lime, nor should I fear to experiment with a little powdered white hellebore.

STRIPED FLEA-BEETLE.

Haltica striolata, Fabr. Family, *Chrysomelidæ*. Sub-Order, *Coleoptera*.

There is a flea-beetle, too (*Haltica striolata*, Fabr.), which I have found to puncture the leaves of cabbages, and is thus quite destructive to young plants. It also works on radishes, turnips, etc.

NATURAL HISTORY.

This beetle is of a shining black color, with two waving lines of buff along the back, one on each side, is very small, less than one-tenth of an inch in length, but is so active, briskly leaping away at the least disturbance, that though so small it can hardly escape notice (Fig. 12.) These beetles often fairly swarm on young plants, and at such times do considerable damage.

FIG. 12.

REMEDIES.

In England, where a nearly related beetle has long given annoyance by attacking cruciferous plants, lime, soot, and even ashes are recommended as securing the plants against the ravages of these pests. I have tried these remedies, but without perfect success. Still, I think they are to be recommended. Anything which promotes vigor of growth is, of course, desirable, for vigorous plants are far less liable to suffer destruction.

By sweeping a fine gauze net over the plants, large numbers of the insects may be caught and destroyed.

OTHER CABBAGE MOTHS.

I might speak of the larvæ of various moths which feed on the leaves of the cabbage, but as there are none in our State sufficiently numerous, so far as I am informed, to do any great damage, and as this report is only to deal with the practical, and as hand-picking is a sure, if it is sometimes a tedious remedy, in all such cases, I will not delay at this time to go into details as to these several species.

CABBAGE FLY.

So, too, I might discuss the cabbage maggot, *Anthomyia brassicæ*, Bouche, but this, as also the onion maggot (*Anthomyia ceparum*, see Fig 13), both of which are in our State, are so similar to the radish fly and maggot (*Anthomyia raphani*) that what I shall say as to the natural history, habits, and remedies of that species, will apply to both of the others.

FIG. 13.

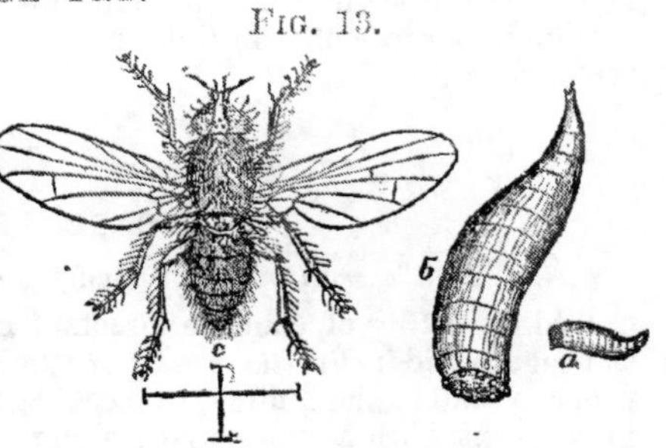

a larva, natural size: *b* same magnified; *c* imago. The lines beneath show the natural size.

RAPE BUTTERFLY.

Pieris rapæ, Schrank. Family, *Papilionidæ*. Sub Order, *Lepidoptera*.

In describing the rape butterfly, I shall depart from my usual practice at this time, and describe an insect not yet among us, for though not a practical subject with us yet, it is likely soon to be, as this latest arrival from England is fast nearing our own beloved State, and without doubt will soon be one of the worst pests of our gardens. What would we think of a report of like design, to be published in Massachusetts, that should fail to give the fullest practical information as to the Colorado potato beetle?

HISTORY IN THE UNITED STATES.

This species, imported from England, was first taken around Quebec, in 1859, since which time, according to Canadian authorities, it has destroyed annually, about Quebec alone, $240,000 worth of cabbages. From thence it has spread rapidly to the south and west, and has already reached western New York, and perhaps even now is entering our own State.

FIG. 14.

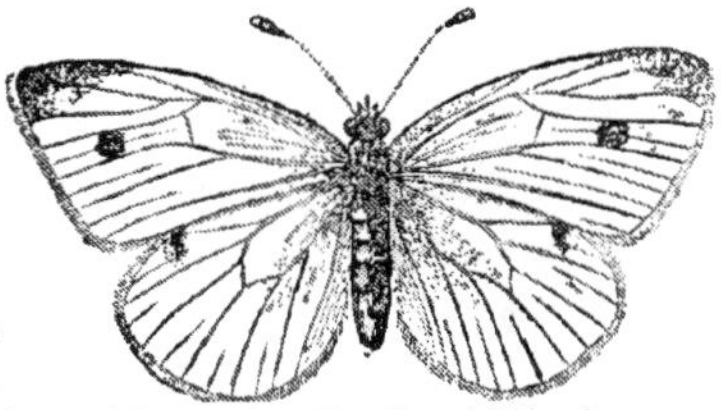

DESCRIPTION.

This butterfly is white, spotted with black, resembling very much our old speckled white cabbage butterfly (*Pieris protodice*, Boisd.), though, as will be seen by the figures (Fig. 14, male, Fig. 15, female), the spots are better defined, while usually there is less black.

FIG. 15.

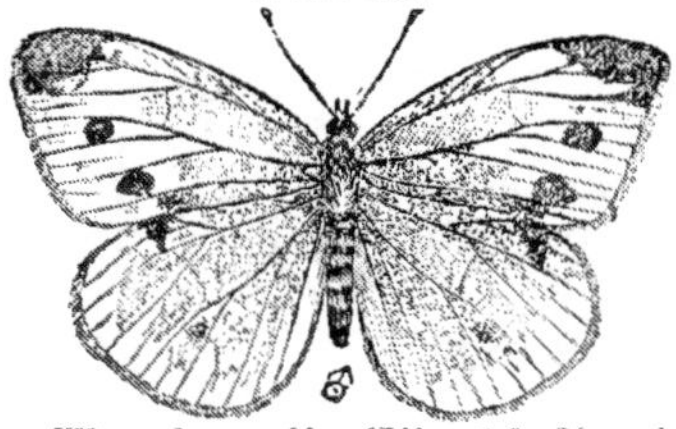

This larvæ (Fig. 16, *a*) is pale green, finely dotted with black, and when mature, one and one-half inches in length, while the larvæ of our old spotted butterfly is blue, striped with yellow.

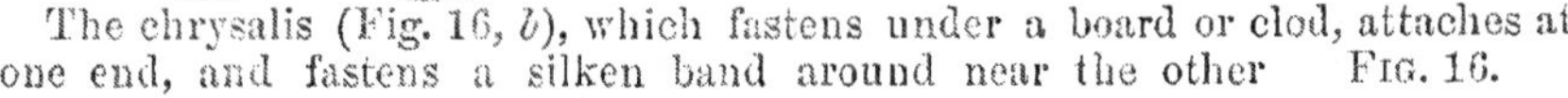

The chrysalis (Fig. 16, *b*), which fastens under a board or clod, attaches at one end, and fastens a silken band around near the other extremity. It is brown, while the old one is gray. I am thus particular in this description, as it is imperative, that we may know the enemy at the first onset, so as to give quick battle.

NATURAL HISTORY.

These butterflies, like both species of our common white ones, are two-brooded. The first butterflies appear early in spring,—in April or May. After pairing, the eggs are deposited on the under side of the cabbage leaves. These hatch, and the larvæ feed on the leaves, assume the chrysalis state, and the imagoes come forth again in June or July. The second brood behave similarly, except that they remain as pupa or chrysalids through the winter.

FIG. 16.

a larva; *b* chrysalis.

REMEDIES.

As these butterflies are slow fliers they may be caught in a net, and thus the whole evil nipped in the bud. Perhaps it would be well to collect the eggs,—the larvæ could be picked off,—but the easiest method is to make use of their habit of pupating beneath a board or other object. By keeping the cabbage patch free from rubbish, which every neat gardener would do any way, and then placing boards horizontally above the ground a few inches, letting them rest on banks of earth ; or better, nailing them to perpendicular boards of the same width, like a common bench. These, distributed among the cabbages, will form a resort for the larvæ in which they will become chrysalids. These chrysalids should then be gathered and destroyed. Were these measures to be generally adopted, we should make short work of a prospective insect evil of the first magnitude.

The evil from the cabbage butterfly is likely to be greatly mitigated among us by a parasite which also pupates in the pupa skin of the butterfly. No pupa containing these should be destroyed.

THE RADISH FLY.

Anthomyia raphani, Haw. Family, *Muscidæ*. Sub-Order, *Diptera*.

The various species of this genus are very annoying in our State, and especially so on sandy soils. In the spring, when we so long for fresh vegetables, and feel our mouths fairly water in prospect of the beautiful tender radishes, it is almost as disheartening as a bank failure to find that the coveted morsels are all ruined by a disgusting maggot.

NATURAL HISTORY.

The small, ash-colored flies, very like the onion fly (Fig. 13), doubtless hibernate, though some may pass the winter as pupæ. However this may be, the flies are around early in the spring, for our earliest radishes are the ones most liable to suffer from attacks. The eggs are laid on the stem close to the ground. These soon hatch, and the whitish, footless, conical larvæ, very like the onion maggot (Fig. 13), feed on the roots, forming grooves all over its surface, which induces decay, and renders the roots unfit for use. In June they transform to pupæ and to imagos, and are ready to make a new deposit of eggs. Hence we see why our early radishes are so very liable to attack, while later ones are often free from injury; though some years none seem to escape. Whether there are more than two broods a year, and whether they attack other plants than radishes, are, so far as I know, still open questions.

REMEDIES.

The late Dr. Walsh recommended hot water as fatal to these maggots, and harmless to the plants. I have tried this with some, though not satisfactory success.

Planting late, or planting on clayey soil, seems advantageous.

Dr. Fitch recommends wide distance between successive radish beds as beneficial. My own experience does not sustain this opinion. It is very desirable to find some application that will render the young plant obnoxious to the fly, thus preventing egg-laying, and yet be harmless to the plant. Who will discover such a compound? These same remarks will apply equally well to the onion and cabbage maggots.

BLISTER BEETLES.

Lytta cinerea, Fabr., and *Lytta attrata*, Fabr. Family, *Meloidæ*. Sub-Order, *Coleoptera*.

These soft-shell, long-necked, trim beetles, the one ash-colored (Fig. 17, *a*), the other coal-black (Fig. 17, *b*), are frequently very injurious to various vegetables and flowers. They sometimes attack beans and asters, and make quick work of whatever falls a prey to their voracious habits.

Fig. 17.

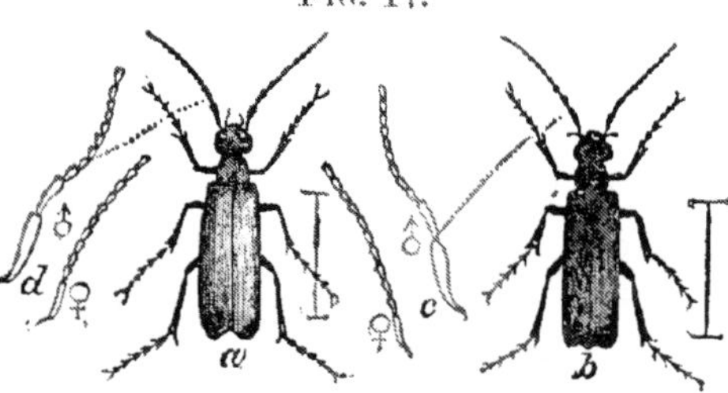

c male and female antennæ of *b*; *d* same of *a*

NATURAL HISTORY.

The larval condition of these beetles has been unknown or involved in doubt. It is supposed that they feed on the roots of grass and other plants.

The beetles appear in early summer and in autumn, and are very voracious feeders.

REMEDIES.

These beetles have the habit of falling off of the plants whenever the latter are suddenly jarred, so in case the plants are tall enough to receive a sheet beneath, or can be bent over an umbrella, the beetles may be readily gathered, and then destroyed by scalding or crushing.

THE STRIPED CUCUMBER BEETLE.

Fig. 18.

Diabrotica vittata, Fabr. Family, *Chrysomelidæ*. Sub-Order, *Coleoptera*.

This beautiful little beetle, yellow with black stripes (Fig. 18), which seems suddenly to fairly swarm on the cucumber and melon vines, is often the cause of great vexation to the gardener.

NATURAL HISTORY.

The larvæ (1, Fig. 18) feed on the roots and underground stems, mature in about a month, pupate in the ground, in which state they continue about two weeks, when the imagos appear. There are two broods a year, and may be three. It passes the winter in the pupa state. The first imagos of the season attack the young vines, and in a single day may destroy them utterly. The later insects do not do so much damage, as the vines, from increased growth, are able to stand the attack.

Fig. 18.

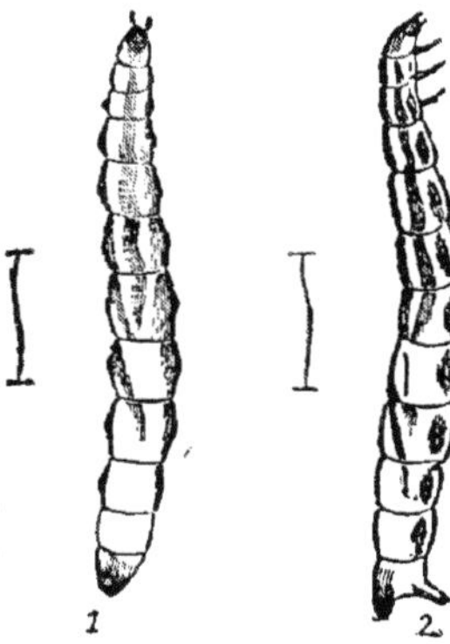

1 2

REMEDIES.

Boxes covered with glass or millinet and placed over the vines are sure protection, providing the beetles do not get inside. If glass is used, care must be taken to shade from the hot sunshine, or the plants may be ruined. These will form miniature hot-beds, and will hasten growth if rightly managed.

Paris green is a certain preventive, and in careful hands is harmless to the vines. I have used this remedy with the very best success. I would put one part green to six parts flour, apply when the vines are dry, and add just as little as I could and see it on the vines. Add a little too much, and the vines are sure to be killed.

THE CODLING MOTH.

Carpocapsa pomonella. Linn. Family, *Tortricidæ.* Sub-Order, *Lepidoptera.*

All will concede that this insect holds first rank among our insect pests.

NATURAL HISTORY.

Fig. 19.

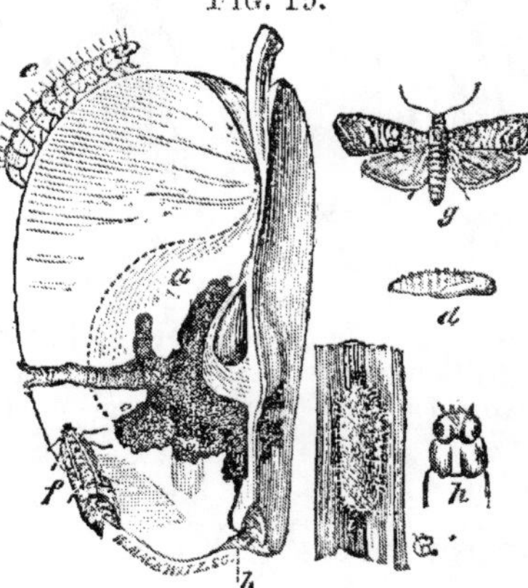

a work in apple; *b* place of entrance; *d* pupa; *e* larva; *f* and *g* imagos; *h* head of larva; *i* cocoon.

The little gray moths (Fig. 16, *f* and *g*) come forth in May and June, are wholly nocturnal, and therefore seldom seen. As soon as the fruit forms, a single egg is laid on the blossom end of the fruit (Fig 19, *b*) and as soon as the egg hatches the larva (Fig. 19, *e*) enters the apple. All know the subsequent history of the larva in the fruit, for who has not seen the tiny white caterpillar, with its black head, mining away at the rich pulp, which it replaces with filth? In three weeks the larva matures, leaves the apple, and in some concealed place spins a silken cocoon (Fig. 19, *i*) and assumes the chrysalis state (Fig. 19, *d*). In from nine to fifteen days, varying with the temperature, the moth issues. The apples are again stocked with eggs as before, after which comes a recurrence of all the disgusting work narrated above, except that the larvæ, upon leaving the apple, simply spin cocoons, in which they remain till spring, when they pupate; and in about two weeks the first moths appear.

The time when the first moths come forth varies from May 1 till July 1; so that moths will be issuing from May 1 till August 1, and the "worms" will be leaving the apples from the last of June till the fruit is gathered. My own experience seems to show that no pupæ are formed after the last week of August, as, so far as I have examined, all larvæ that leave the apple after that time simply spin a cocoon, in which they remain in larvæ till the next spring. Some of the observing fruit men of our State think that during the past season many of these insects pupated after that time. Such cases come not within my observation.

Of those larvæ which leave the apple while it still hangs in the tree, about one half crawl down, till beneath some bark or in some crevice they find seclusion in which to spin unobserved. Those which fall to the ground with the fruit crawl out; and if the ground is free from all rubbish, stumps, etc., they crawl up the tree and hide as before.

REMEDIES.

Place around the trunk of every bearing tree, midway between the ground and branches, a woolen cloth about five inches wide, and sufficiently long to pass around and lap enough to tack. This may be fastened with one or two tacks. I have usually found one placed in the middle to be quite sufficient. The tack should not be driven quite up to the head. Before the cloth band is adjusted the loose bark should be scraped off. This may be done earlier in the season, when time will best permit. The bands should be adjusted by June 20. Under these bands the "worms" will secrete themselves. By July 7 the bands around the earliest apple-trees should be unwound and examined, and the larvæ destroyed. This can be done by passing the bands through a wringer, or by unwinding and crushing with the thumb. I have found this last method the best. Every ten days after the first round—every nine days if the weather is dry and warm—this work should be repeated, till the last week of August, and again at the close of the season after the fruit is gathered. A common carpet-tack hammer, with a good claw, suspended around the neck by a cord, will be found an advantage.

Many apples will be carried to the cellar with the larvæ still in them. These larvæ, unless destroyed, will go through their changes. Hence, all barrels, bins, and boxes in the cellar should be examined. In knocking a box to pieces a few days ago (March 13), procured from a neighbor's cellar, I found over 100 larvæ concealed where the boards were nailed together. These were placed in a box, and all but two again spun cocoons. As we cannot hope to find nearly all of these, it would be well if the apple cellar were so arranged as to preclude the moths from issuing forth. It would be excellent policy to have our cellars so close that not a moth could escape in May and June. Were all cellars so fixed this spring it would be a great benefit, for I can find no live larvæ out in the orchards. In examining an orchard last week (April 27) I found over 100 cocoons. From more than one-third of these the insects had been taken by the sap-sucker (*Picus villosus*), while all the others, either from cold or some other cause were dead. I never saw such codling moth mortality before this spring. Fires and jars of sweetened water will have no effect in destroying these moths, as I have proved that neither attract them. Hogs turned into the orchard are but a partial remedy, as at least half of the larvæ never go to the ground at all.

OLD APPLE-TREE BORER.

Saperda candida, Fab. Family *Cerambycidæ*. Sub-Order *Coleoptera*.

This pest, which has been so long in our country, is widely distributed in our State. Very few if any orchards are exempt from its attacks. Not that it always, or generally, totally destroys the trees; still, those suffering from its attacks are always lessened in vitality, and it not unfrequently happens that the trunks become so riddled with their tunnels that the tree becomes a prey to the hard winds, which are sure to come with each returning year.

NATURAL HISTORY.

The beautiful brown beetle (Fig. 20, *c*), with its two stripes of white, appears early in June, and thence on through July. So the egg-laying is principally done in these two months. The grub (Fig. 20, *a*), whitish with a round black head, eats through the bark, and then usually passes in and up, frequently eating through the branches far out towards the extremity. I have frequently found

Fig. 20.

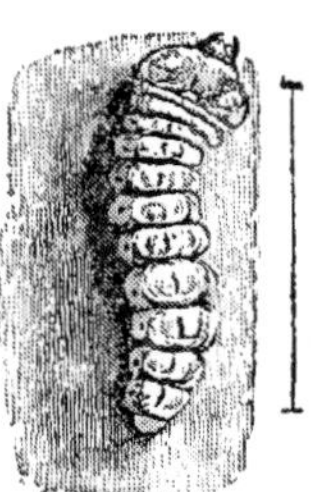

a

b

c

apple-tree limbs no larger than my thumb, with a tunnel as large as a pipe-stem. These larvæ push their sawdust-like particles back of them and out of the hole where they first entered, so that it is not difficult to find them. They live and feed on the wood of the tree for three years; hence we see how that a single larvæ may bore, if left undisturbed, for a distance of several feet. They finally bore a hole for exit, fill it slightly with their sawdust, and a little back of the same make a cocoon of their own chips, in which they pupate (Fig. 20, *b*). Soon after, in June and July, the beetles again appear.

REMEDIES.

Soapy mixtures are found to be obnoxious to these beetles, so that in their egg-laying they are found to avoid trees to which such an application has been made. Thus we may hope to escape all danger by washing the smooth trunks of our trees early in June, and again early in July, with soft soap or a very strong solution of the same. T. T. Lyon, now of South Haven, whose judgment is very reliable in such matters, urges that we always use the soap itself.

We should always examine the trees carefully in September, and wherever we find this pernicious grub's sawdust shingle out, we should give him a call. Perhaps we may reach him with a wire thrust into the hole, and by a vigorous ramming crush the culprit. If we have doubts as to the crushing, we should follow him with a knife; but in cutting out the borers, too great care cannot be taken to wound the tree just as little as possible. This heroic method is sure, and requires very little time, and no person who takes pride in his orchard, or looks to it as a source of profit, can afford to neglect this September examination, nor the previous application of soap to which it is supplementary.

THE FLAT-HEADED BORER.

Chrysobothris femorata, Fab. Family, *Buprestidæ*. Sub-Order, *Hemiptera*.

At present this borer is quite as ruinous in our State as the preceding one, and I should not think it strange if in a well balanced account it was found even to surpass the other in the evil which it works to our fruit interests. I have seen young orchards nearly ruined the first summer after setting, by this devastator. Not long since a nurseryman came from a distant part of the State to consult me as to the ravages of this pest. He said that during the past summer, in some regions of the State, more than half the trees he sold were killed by this scourge, and of course he was unjustly blamed. At present, no nurseryman should sell trees without throwing in advice in regard to protecting against this devastator; for, as we shall see, such trees are peculiarly liable to attack.

These borers are not confined to the apple-trees, as I have found them working in oak, maple, and other trees of our forests.

NATURAL HISTORY.

This brownish beetle (Fig 21), with a coppery luster, is found from May till August, though I have found them more common in June and July. As with the striped *Saperda*, the eggs are laid on the bark. The whitish grubs (Fig. 22), with their enormous front, brown head, and curled tail, usually bore only superficially, eating the inner bark and sap-wood; yet I have seen, and have now on exhibition here at the college, sections of young trees over an inch in diameter, bored completely through by these big-headed rascals. They eat but a single

FIG. 21.

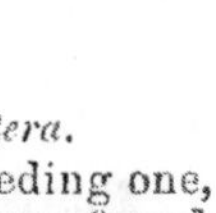

season, pupate as in the preceding case, and come forth as imagos early in the spring.

They usually work on the trunk, though sometimes in the branches, almost always on the south, the west, or the southwest sides of the tree; and their whereabouts may always be ascertained, not only by the sawdust, but also, and more certainly, by the black color of the bark. When the black color offers the suggestion of the presence of this borer, we can quickly become assured by striking a knife into the same. If the blade pierces the bark and goes on still a little further, we may be sure of the enemy's presence.

Fig. 22.

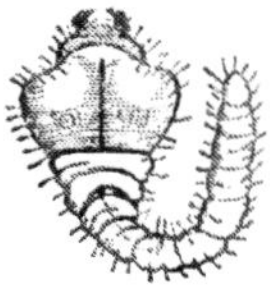

This borer is far more liable to attack feeble trees. Anything, therefore, which serves to diminish the vitality of the trees, promotes the ravages of this borer. Hence, after such a winter as we have just experienced, or after having the growth of our trees interrupted by the removal from the nursery to our orchards, we are in special danger of harm from these destructive borers. Hence, the coming season, when loss will be inevitable, we should more than ever be on the alert to mitigate the damage by our vigilance and care, and by the timely application of

REMEDIES.

The remedies for the flat-headed borer are the same as those given for the old borer,—soap in June and July, and a knife in September,—though these grubs may be found in July and August, and to delay the cutting out till September would often be fatal, especially to trees in newly set orchards. I have known cases where labor of this kind in July would have paid more than $100 a day, besides saving a great amount of vexation.

APPLE-TREE BARK LOUSE.

Mytilaspis conchiformis, Gmelin. Family, *Coccidæ*. Sub-Order, *Hemiptera*.

This old enemy, though less destructive than formerly (probably because of parasites and mites which prey upon it, so that, like the Hessian fly, wheat midge, and many other insects, it has probably done its worst work), yet, to leave it to itself at the present time would be to yield the strife prematurely.

NATURAL HISTORY.

The bark-colored, oblong scales (Fig. 23), so harmless in appearance, serve from August to May only for protection to the 60 or 70 wee white eggs (1, Fig. 24) which are found underneath. About the first of June the young lice (2, Fig. 24) appear,—so small that, though clad in yellow, they can hardly be seen without a glass. Coming forth from under the scale, they roam about for a few days,—are sometimes blown to other trees, thus spreading their evil work,—but very soon settle down to earnest business. This consists in inserting their tiny beak and sucking the vitality from the trees. Very soon a scale (3, 4, 5, and 6, Fig. 24, different stages of development of scale) commences to form around them, from an exudation which is a secretion from the general surface. By August the impervious scale is complete (7, Fig. 24,). The eggs are then soon deposited, and the parent louse

Fig. 23.

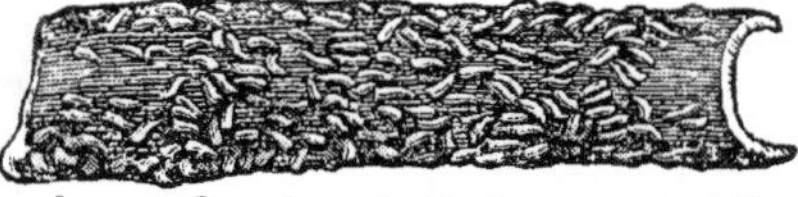

dries up and shrinks away to nothingness.

Fig. 24.

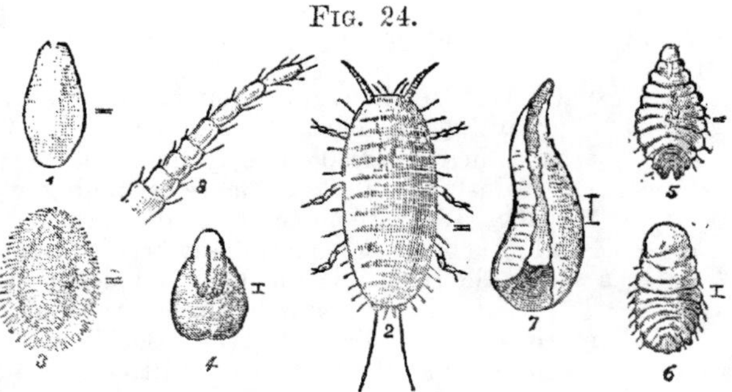

REMEDIES.

As the scale is impervious to most fluids, though oils will penetrate it and destroy the eggs, the best time to fight these insects is just after the eggs hatch. At this time, soft soap or strong soap suds are sure death to the young lice. Hence, the trees should be washed the first week of June with soft soap, not only making the application to the trunk, but also to the main branches and limbs so far as possible.

IMPORTANT FACT.

We thus see that an application of soft soap to our apple trees, made the first week of June, is of exceeding value. It not only exterminates the sappers (bark lice), but banishes the miners (borers). We thus understand why our fruit trees which are thus treated seem fairly to laugh, as if grateful for such timely aid in banishing their enemies. I have no hesitation in affirming that the apple-grower will find the above one of the most paying operations that he can undertake in his orchard. Let all, then, scrape their trees early in spring, apply soft soap—not lye—the first of June, and again the first of July, not forgetting to adjust cloth bands by the last of June.

TWIG-BORERS.

Bostrichus bicaudatus, Say. Family, *Ptinidæ*. Sub-Order, *Coleoptera*.

It will have been noticed during the past summer, that in very many portions of our State the twigs of the fruit trees, especially apple and pear trees, would wilt, die, and often break off. This is caused by two insects: the twig-borer, named above, and even more by the insect to be next mentioned.

HABITS.

The twig-borer does not bore as a larvæ, as do most beetles, but the imago or mature insect, in this case, does the damage. Both males and females are found in about equal proportions in the twigs. The beetles are small, dark brown, and the males can easily be told from the females by their bodies terminating in small spines (Fig. 25).

Fig. 25.

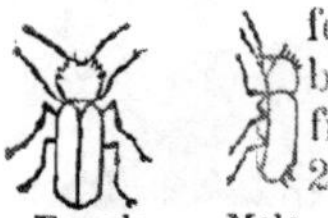

Female. Male.

They bore into a twig just above a bud (Fig. 26, *c*), and work down through the pith for two inches, thus causing the branch or twig to wither and die. The tunnel (Fig. 26, *d*) is about the size of a large knitting needle.

Fig. 26.

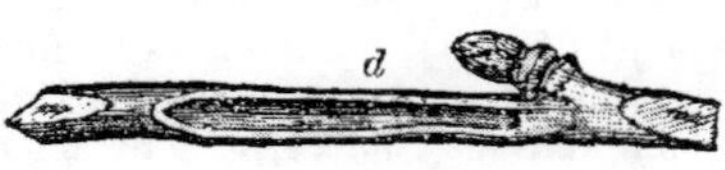

REMEDIES.

Cut off the twigs as soon as noticed and burn them.

TWIG-PRUNER.

Elaphidium parallelum, Newm. Family, *Cerambycidæ*. Sub-Order, *Coleoptera*.

During the past season there has been very general complaint throughout the State of limbs of apple, pear, and plum trees dying and falling off. From branches sent me by John Suttle of Grand Rapids, Mr. Sneathan, South Boston, and others, I have bred the above named insect.

NATURAL HISTORY.

In spring, the brown beetle, well covered with yellowish hairs, with trim body and graceful antennæ (Fig. 27, *c*), lays its eggs. These are placed in the axle of the leaves, usually in small twigs near the extremity of the limbs. Upon hatching, the grub (Fig. 27, *a*) bores into the twig and on towards the body of the tree. In July the limbs will show disease. The larvæ mature in the fall, so cut the limb that it may be easily broken, and assume the pupa state in the burrow (Fig. 27, *b*). These branches are quite apt to be carried to the ground by the autumn winds. During the winter or early spring the insect changes to the mature state, though in our warm rooms this may occur in mid-winter; and thus the beetle is ready to commence another season's operations.

FIG. 27.

This insect, in its, size, habits, and appearance, bears a very striking resemblance to the oak-pruner (*E. villosus*, Fab.), so long and so well known in our State.

REMEDIES.

The remedies are the same as for the twig-borer, though there is not the same danger in delay as with the former. If it were really known that the offenders were the pruners, and this can be easily determined by breaking open a twig during the summer when first attacked,—if the beetle is found it is the twig-borer, if a "worm" it is the pruner,—we might delay action till fall and be sure to get them. But it would be safest to cut and burn the twig so soon as it gave indication of the destroyer. In this course we should be sure to nip both evils, and so nearly in the bud that very much less damage will ensue, in case of the pruner, than though we delay operations till autumn, when our labor will only be repaid by lessening the danger for the next year. We must not confound with the work of these borers the twig blight, which is doing great damage in our State and Canada the present season. This blight, which bids fair to be a serious plague, may be readily distinguished, as the closest scrutiny shows no marks of an insect.

CANKER WORM.

Anisopteryx vernata, Peck. Family, *Phalænidæ*. Sub-Order, *Lepidoptera*.

This insect has a curious history in our State; for though it has made its appearance several times, once in Calhoun county, again in Genesee county and in other places, for the past two or three years near Commerce, Oakland county, and just now near Pontiac, of the same county,* still it has never

* Mr. M. W. Gray, near Pontiac, has just sent me some veritable canker worms, with the remark that his orchard is suffering severely, and that his neighbors are very anxious. Still later, I received specimens of this same insect, sent by H. P. Harris of Adrian to Mr. Chas. Betts, the able agricultural editor of the Detroit Tribune, who forwarded them, together with Mr. Harris' letter, to me. The insects come from the orchard of Mr. R. M. Baily, and are accompanied by the usual story of despoliation and ruin.

seemed to hold on; for, after destroying a few orchards, it seems to succumb to natural enemies, or unpropitious circumstances, and ceases to cause even anxiety. That it will be but a temporary evil among us is perhaps asserting too much, yet I think it a plausible supposition; and it is certainly earnestly to be hoped. Our New England friends have had to fight this insect for many years, and it seems no less a pest to-day than ever before, except as a better knowledge of its habits makes it easier to ward off its injuries.

NATURAL HISTORY.

The wingless female moth (Fig. 28,*b*), and the trim male (Fig. 28, *a*), with his ample wings, both gray or ash color, the female being a little the darker, come forth from the ground early in the spring: I have often seen the males during warm winter days. The female crawls up the trunks of the apple-trees, and after meeting the male, lays her cluster of eggs (Fig. 29, *b*), often to the number of one hundred. If the female fails for any reason to gain acces to the tree, she fastens these egg clusters to any convenient object. I have often seen them in Cambridge, Massachusetts, fastened to the pickets or boards of fences. After egg-laying these insects soon die. Just as the leaves begin to burst forth, the larvæ (Fig. 29, *a*) begin to come forth. The larvæ (Fig. 29, *a*) vary very much in color. At first they are very dark, with faint yellowish stripes. When full-grown they are striped with ash color, black, and yellow, and are about one inch in length. These larvæ belong to the loopers, or measuring worms, both names referring to their peculiar method of locomotion. They do not have the usual number of legs for caterpillars (16), but must be content with only ten. Hence their looping gait. They are also called drop worms, because of the habit of swinging from the tree by a thread when disturbed, or when they desire to go to the ground to pupate. As they are often seen thus suspended, it has been supposed that they frequently swing just for the pleasure of the thing. It may be that some disturbing wind or bird induced this strange manœuvre.

FIG. 28.

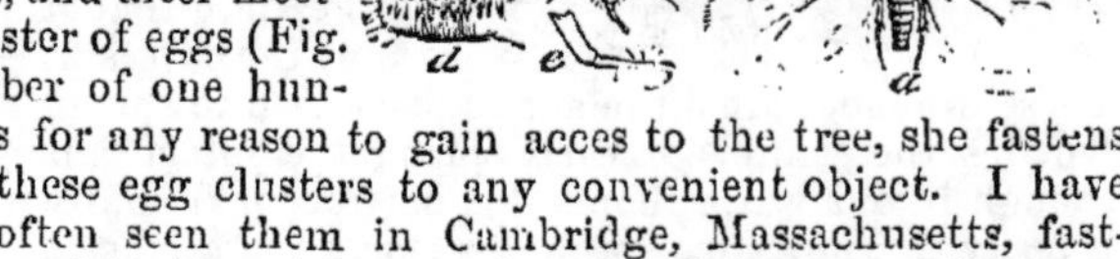

FIG. 29.

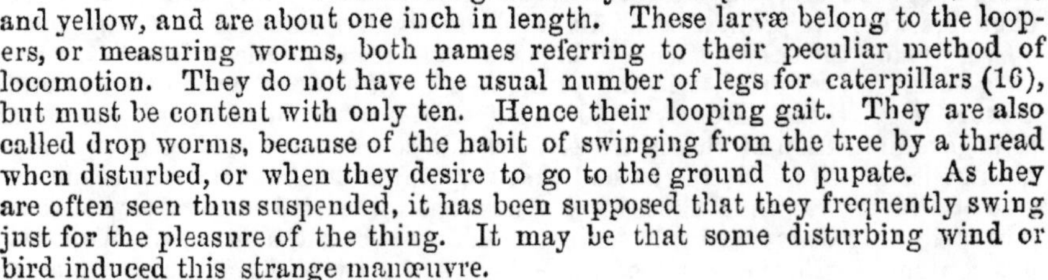

About the middle of June the larvæ are full fed, the tree fully denuded of its foliage, and that, too, at the worst possible time, the growing season, when the "worms" make for the ground, some creeping down the trunk, others dropping down by a silken thread spun for the purpose. Upon reaching the ground they burrow to the depth of four or five inches, and in an earthen cocoon change to pupæ. The chrysalis is of a light brown color, and smaller for male than for female.

This destructive insect is not content to injure the apple-tree alone, but is equally ready to attack the elm, and not infrequently attacks cherry, plum, and other fruit and forest trees.

REMEDIES.

As prevention is better than cure, we ought, of course, whenever possible, to keep injurious insects from even gaining a foothold; and the wingless condition of this female moth permits us to accomplish this, as she must ascend the tree in order to work injury. Any substance which prevents this will prevent the defoliation. The old method so long practiced in New England is to closely surround the tree with paper bands, say eight inches wide, and besmear the bands with tar or printer's ink. This gives the trees a forbidding appearance, and necessitates renewed application of the adhesive substance so frequently as to be sure that we entrap the moth as she attempts to pass up the tree. Dr. Le Baron suggests a neater and, he says, an effectual remedy. He would place an inch rope closely around the tree, letting it lap a little so as to be sure to entirely surround the tree. Then tack the rope to the tree at each end. Now take a strip of tin, say five inches wide, place it around over the rope so that the rope shall be just in the middle of the tin; lap this a little and tack to the rope. It is said that the female moths, coming up to the rope and being unable to crawl through under the tin, will crawl around and get on to the tin, but that they will never get from the tin to the tree again. Upon reaching the top of the tin they pass round and round, not knowing that they can pass down and thus gain their desired end. Like turkeys entrapped in a pen whose only exit is through a hole beneath the earth's level, they are balked through sheer stupidity. In this case the moths will doubtless lay eggs around and below the tins. These can be destroyed by using kerosene oil. This, turned upon the eggs, destroys them. Eggs laid in close proximity to the trees or wherever seen, can be destroyed in the same way.

If the moths once gain access to the tree, and the larvæ commence their work of despoliation, we can take advantage of their dropping propensity and destroy them. Place a little straw under the tree, not sufficient to injure it when burned. Then jar the tree, and as the larvæ swing down by their threads bring them upon the straw by sweeping the threads with a pole, then set fire to the straw, and we are rid of the pests. The only trouble will be to be sure to make them drop. To be complete, this will need cautious pains. During the past year syringing the trees with a mixture of Paris green and water was tried with marked success in Illinois, and is highly recommended by those who tried it.

Though the neighbors of people with affected orchards may take satisfaction in the prospect of a speedy leave-taking of this terrible scourge, still those who have orchards attacked will find that persistent effort in the line marked out above will be the price of their orchards, as two or three years at most will utterly ruin the trees. But this price is not very exorbitant, as the labor is not very great, does not last very long, and is most effectual when applied in the least busy season of all the year.

TENT CATERPILLAR.

Clisiocampa Americana, Harr. Family, *Bombycidæ*. Sub-Order, *Lepidoptera*.

These familiar insects, so sure to fix their silken tents within our trees, come just at the right time to do the greatest harm, and should never be left to their miserable work of despoilation.

NATURAL HISTORY.

These pretty moths (Fig. 30), brown in color, the female a little lighter and larger than the male, with two light bands running obliquely across the fore wings, appear in June and July. For the past four years I have taken the first of these during the first week of July, and those reared in confinement came forth at the same time. These moths, unlike the codling moth, are attracted by lights, and very frequently fly into our rooms during our warm July evenings. After pairing, the female moths lay their eggs (*c*, Fig. 30) in a compact cluster about the small twigs, covering them with a glistening glue, so that they are impervious to water. These eggs,—300 or 400 in a cluster,—hatch just as the leaves of the apple and cherry are putting forth, on both of which trees they are wont to engage in their ruinous work, seeming rather to prefer the wild cherry. They immediately weave their tents, and become conspicuous objects in the orchard. They remain huddled in these tents except when going forth to feed. They are quite regular in taking their meals, and usually all go forth at once. These larvæ or caterpillars (*a* Fig. 30), variously striped with white, yellow, black, and blue, are very handsome, feed voraciously, so that by the middle of June they are not only matured in size,—being now two inches in length,—but have managed to strip the trees pretty thoroughly of their leaves. They then disperse, seeking in all directions for some crevice in which they may form their closely woven cocoons undisturbed and unseen. They

Fig. 30.

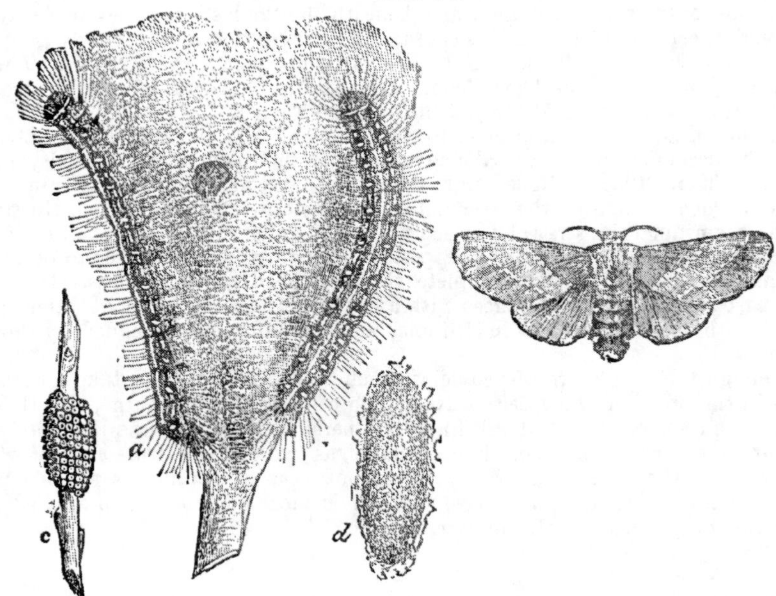

pupate almost immediately. In about two weeks they come forth as moths. And thus, the cycle of growth and change completed, the moth sallies forth to again prepare for future evil.

REMEDIES.

Let no one think, because these pests have been neglected in the past and their trees still live, that such neglect is in the least wise; and if such lose their orchards because of the severe cold of the past winter, let them blame only themselves. No tree can receive such shocks without materially lessening their vitality, and though they may not die outright, the seeds of premature death are sown, and the power to survive severe winters or continuous drouths is materially weakened.

It is often recommended to examine the trees on sunshiny days of winter and spring, when the glistening egg clusters will catch the eye, and may be gathered and destroyed. Yet I doubt if this will prove best. It takes too long to find them, even on bright days, and even then many will be missed. Besides, much time will be spent in seeking in trees where no clusters exist.

I think the best method is to destroy the young larvæ so soon as the tents appear in the trees, and before any harm is done. At this time they are easily found, and none need be missed. If this is done when the larvæ are not feeding, they will all be compactly clustered in the tent, and can be quickly dispatched. There are various methods by which to accomplish the slaughter. I think the safest and perhaps the best is to crush them with the hand. This may not be exactly to the taste, but with an old pair of gloves, the delicacy, I think, will be but transient. Another method is to put a light charge of powder into a gun, and, holding the muzzle immediately against the tent, discharge the piece. This requires much caution or the tree will be injured. Another method is to burn them with a torch fastened to a long pole; and still another to kill them by an application of strong soap suds, or a weak solution of petroleum, applied with a swab, on a long pole. The objection to all these last is the danger of not being thorough, and of injuring the trees.

A year or two since I gave before the State Pomological Society Dr. Fitch's suggestion, to set wild cherry trees around the orchard. These would attract the insects, and, all being in a few trees, could be more easily destroyed. The idea was generally denounced by those present, but close attention since that time has confirmed me in the opinion that the idea is a good one. The insects will attack something, and preferring the cherry leaves, will take those in preference. Thus they are drawn from the orchard, and in case of neglect will leave our more valuable trees uninjured; and if killed, as they should be, it can be done in the more confined space far more quickly.

Last summer I observed a large orchard where, in the surrounding fence corners, were about a dozen cherry trees. These were full of tents, while the orchard was almost entirely free. Other orchards within a mile were great sufferers.

FALL WEB-WORM.

Hyphantria textor, Harr. Family, *Bombycidæ*. Sub-Order, *Lepidoptera*.

The habits of these insects are in some respects like those of the preceding, and it is doubtless this fact that has led some able fruit men to believe what is entirely erroneous, that the tent caterpillar is double-brooded. These fall web worms, though unsightly, are far from being as destructive as the tent caterpillar. The leaves, at the time of their arrival, have so far performed their mission, that for the tree to be robbed of them is not generally fatal, though of course the condition of the tree is enfeebled.

FIG. 31.

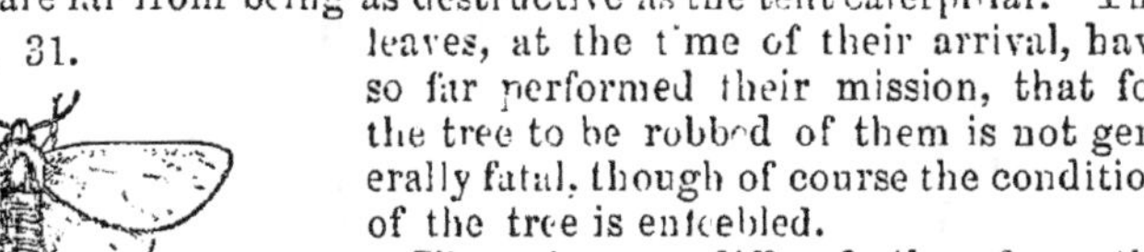

These insects differ farther from the tent caterpillar in being indiscriminate feeders. Nearly every variety of tree has to contribute to their support.

NATURAL HISTORY.

The beautiful white moths (Fig. 31, *c*) lay their eggs in clusters upon the leaves. These hatch in July and August, when the larvæ (Fig. 31, *a*) immediately spin their web and feed in companies, though instead of eating the entire leaf they only feed on the upper skin and pulp. They thus continue, spreading their unsightly webs, eating the leaves, till full grown, when they are an inch in length. These little "worms" are very beautiful, being striped with yellow and black, and dotted with orange. In September and October they descend from the tree, and in the ground or some crevice spin very thin cocoons in which the pupa (Fig. 31, *b*) soon appears. It remains thus till the next June, when the beautiful white, immaculate moth, expanding a little over an inch, appears.

REMEDIES.

These must needs be destroyed in the larvæ state, and the same methods may be employed as those given for conquering the tent caterpillar. As they always feed in their webs, sometimes we may safely and wisely cut the limb off on which they have spread their web. Of course we should commence operations as soon as the insects do, as shown by the newly formed webs.

PLANT LICE.

Aphides. Family, *Aphidæ.* Sub-Order, *Hemiptera.*

As plant lice, some species of which attack nearly every kind of plant, are so preyed upon by natural enemies that they are of little importance as enemies to out-door plants, I shall not discuss them in detail, only remarking that tobacco water, whale oil soap solution, or a weak solution of petroleum, will destroy them. Care is requisite in using the last, or the plants will be destroyed. Ants in trees are almost certain evidence of the presence of the lice, the ants being present to sip the sweets which exude from the lice.

PLUM CURCULIO.

Conotrachelus nenuphar, Herbst. Family, *Curculionidæ.* Sub-Order, *Coleoptera.*

This little beetle, though so small, certainly ranks very high as an orchard pest. It is he that has almost banished plum culture in our State. It is he that ruins our cherries, often by wholesale. It is he that has a tooth for the luscious peach; and unless prevented, materially lessens the profits. And even our king of fruits, the apple, is frequently made to contribute to the support of the little Turk. His presence in wind-fall apples has misled some good observers into thinking that the codling-moth larvæ had worked slightly on the apple and then left it. If this report could induce the restoration of plum culture in our State, by showing how easily we can secure our crops, it would pay its cost a million times over.

HABITS.

The curculio (Fig. 32, *c*) hibernates during the winter in the mature state. In early spring, and even later, he lies concealed by day under boards, clods, etc. This weevil is nocturnal, being active at night. So soon as our plums, peaches, and cherries set, the curculio, a little brown beetle, commences operations, imprinting the familiar crescent (Fig. 32, *d*) and placing an egg inside. This egg-laying continues even to July. As the weather becomes warmer the insect forsakes its habit of going down to the ground by day to hide, but remains in the tree. These beetles are not solely engaged in pairing and egg-laying, for they are good feeders and gouge out many a hole in our fruits to satisfy

FIG. 32.

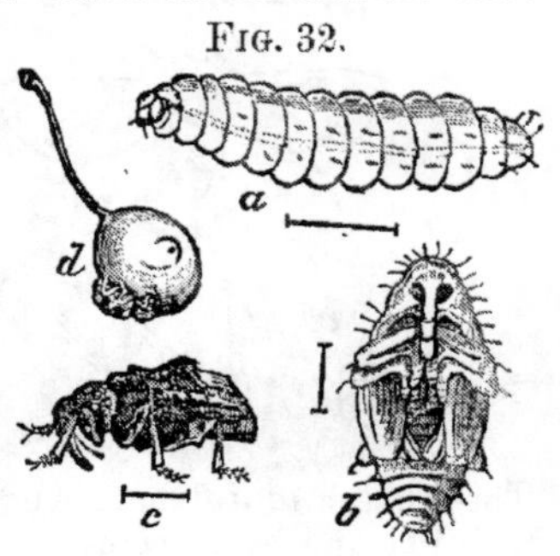

their appetites. The eggs soon hatch, when the young larvæ bore into the fruit and continue to eat. As these are sometimes, though quite rarely, found in apples, I would state that they can be easily told from the codling moth larvæ, as they are without legs, thus resembling maggots. They grow rapidly to maturity (Fig. 32, *a*), thus causing plums, apples, and peaches to fall prematurely, though cherries usually remain on the tree. The earliest larvæ are ready to go into the ground and pupate (Fig. 32, *b*) by the last of June. As egg-laying goes on even till July, it will readily be seen that larvæ will be found in the fruit all through the summer, and I have found them in peaches even in September. All of these pupæ change into mature insects during summer and autumn, so the insects all pass the winter as mature beetles, concealed either under boards, or in crevices, or even in the ground. In May they commence coming forth, and continue to put in an appearance even to mid-summer. We see, then, that the old disputed question is settled,—that these insects are singled brooded, and that the old notion that they were double brooded, arose from the fact that some are so early, while others are very tardy in coming from their winter retreat; though it may be that those insects that appear so late in our orchards come from other orchards, or even from the forests.

As was said above, these insects are nocturnal, though they will fly in the hot sunshine. Yet they will fly more freely at night, and seem far less timid.

It is a fortunate peculiarity of this beetle to fall from the tree if it is suddenly jarred. In this condition, when it seems to contract itself to the utmost, it has been compared not inaptly to a dried bud.

REMEDIES.

Of late the Ransom process, invented by Mr. Ransom of St. Joseph, has been largely practiced, and has given great satisfaction. It takes advantage of the habit of the insect, early in the season, to hide by day, and consists in keeping the ground beneath and around the trees perfectly clean, and so thoroughly cultivated that it will be perfectly smooth, and placing chips or boards on the ground close about the tree. Mr. Ransom preferred oak bark: pieces of shingles would do. If bark is used the outside should be placed up, and whatever is used, the lower side should be entirely smooth. Three pieces, each the size of the hand, will be quite sufficient for each tree, and may be placed equally distant from each other, close about the base of the trunk. Early in May the beetles will commence to hide under these pieces. So soon as they are found to collect they should be gathered daily, and thence on so long as they are found, even to July. Mr. Dyckman, who claims that this method saves him three hundred dollars annually, in protecting his peach orchard, pursues the following method in gathering the insects. He hires boys to visit the chips daily, taking the curculios in their fingers and putting them in bottles, counting them as they are dropped in the bottles. He then pays them according to the number collected. This makes the boys active, and ensures the destruction of the insects.

Later in the season, it will be remembered, the insects do not go down to hide. Yet Mr. Ransom claims that the chip trap can still be made effectual, and cheaper than any other plan, by the following additional labor. Early in the day, pass through the orchard with a mallet, and give each bearing tree a smart blow. This will cause the insects to fall to the ground, when they will hide as before, and can be gathered into the bottles as before. The taking the insects from under the chips should not be delayed too long, as towards night they commence going into the tree to be in good time for their rascally night work.

While Mr. Ransom claims, and with reason, that the above method is all that is required, still some of our fruit men claim that this process must be supplemented late in the season by the older and more expensive method of jarring the insects on to a sheet. This consists in passing through the orchard, morning or evening, placing under each tree a sheet, and then giving the tree a sharp blow with a mallet, whereupon the insects will fall upon the sheet and can be gathered and destroyed.

The sheet had best be fastened to a frame in the shape of an inverted umbrella, and carried on one or two wheels (Fig. 33), if it is to be used extensively. A slit in the front, opposite the handles, allows the sheet to be brought under the tree. The size of the wheels and the sheet can be adjusted to suit the ideas of the orchardist, and the size of his trees. If there are but few trees, the sheet can be tacked to a frame and carried by two persons. The mallet should be of rubber, so as not to mar the trees, though some saw off a limb or drive in a spike, in which case the blow will cause no injury to the tree. Some prefer to bump the trees with the vehicle which carries the sheet. In this case the vehicle must be strong, and the spike should be driven so that it will not permit the tree to be struck.

Fig. 33.

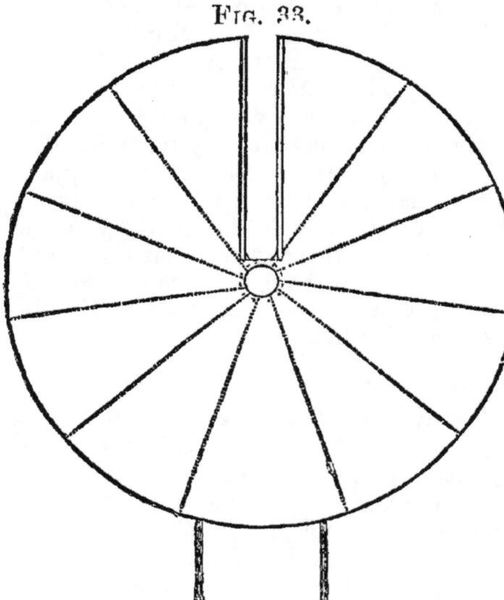

A two-wheel machine seen from above.

In case of a few plum trees, it is well to have chickens confined beneath them. The jarring winds will bring the beetles down, when the chickens will pick them up. There is considerable evidence in favor of this plan. Still, with the present high price of plums, no one can afford to be without these trees; nor can we afford to leave them solely to the care of the fowls, but should always practice the other method which will insure good crops of this luscious fruit, and thus give us a luxury for our tables and money for our pockets.

One of our last year's graduates has had charge the past summer of a plum orchard in Ohio, and has, he writes me, convinced his neighbors by that best convincer, success, that it pays to fight insects on scientific principles.

As many know, we are greatly aided in our attempts to baffle the evil attempts of injurious insects, by a host of parasites, chief among which are the ichneumon flies, which may readily be known by their long, compressed abdomens, and long, excerted ovipositors. It is wonderful, the instinct that guides these instinct destroyers to their enemies. Even the plum curculio, secluded as he is, and seeming so exempt from molestation as a larva, has more than one of these wily foes to cut short his work of destruction.

One of these (Fig. 34), the *Sigalphus curculonis*, Fitch, has been known to work on the curculio for a number of years. The female in the illustration shows the attitude in which the fatal thrust is made. It is very interesting to watch the operation of egg-laying, as I have frequently done, of another ichneumon during the past summer, on our currant "worms."

Fig. 34.

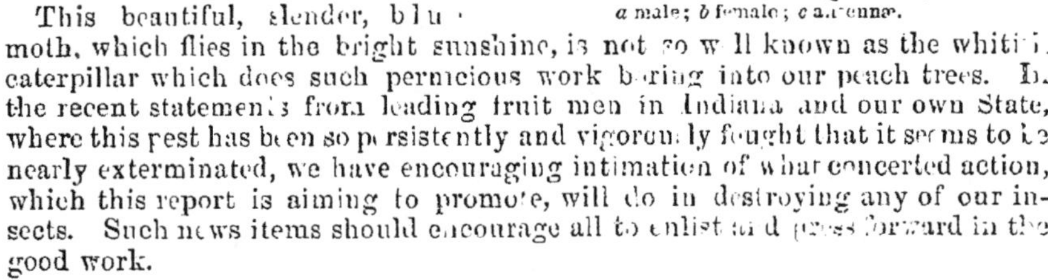

a male; *b* female; *c* antennæ.

PEACH BORER.

Ægeria exitiosa, Say. Family *Ægeriidæ*.
Sub-Order, *Lepidoptera*.

This beautiful, slender, blue moth, which flies in the bright sunshine, is not so well known as the whitish caterpillar which does such pernicious work boring into our peach trees. By the recent statements from leading fruit men in Indiana and our own State, where this pest has been so persistently and vigorously fought that it seems to be nearly exterminated, we have encouraging intimation of what concerted action, which this report is aiming to promote, will do in destroying any of our insects. Such news items should encourage all to enlist and press forward in the good work.

NATURAL HISTORY.

These gay moths (Fig. 35), resembling wasps in appearance, come forth in July, August and September. I have hatched them in all of these months.

Fig. 35.

1 female; 2 male.

They soon pair, and then egg-laying commences. The eggs are laid just at the base of the trunk. Soon after the whitish larvæ will be found, as they have commenced boring in the bark and sapwood, just beneath the surface of the ground. Wherever they work, just beneath the earth will be found a sticky mass, formed of the oozing gum and their chip-dust, which gives quick indication of their presence. These larvæ are found of very varying sizes, which is easily understood, from the fact of the length of time at which the moths come forth, from July to September. These larvæ will be found at work till about the first week of July, when we will often only find pupæ encased in a rough cocoon of chip-dust, earth, and gum. By seeking out these oval cocoons, any one may, by keeping them in earth in a close box, rear the beautiful moths. The female (1, Fig. 35), is larger, darker than the male, and has a bright yellow band across her abdomen. The male (2, Fig. 35), expands about an inch. In hatching a large number, I have found that the ratio of males to females is about one to five, which would seem to indicate that polygamy reigned among insects. In pushing out of their cocoon, the pupa skin is always left projecting from the opening. Perhaps the split cocoon serves them as a vise, thus aiding them to gain their freedom.

REMEDIES.

It has been recommended to mound the trees with earth in summer. Of course the caterpillars will still work near the top of the mound. In fall, say the last of September, these mounds are pulled down, and the hot sun kills the tender-skinned larvæ. There are three objections to this plan: 1st, the mounds interfere with the Ransom process of fighting the curculio; 2d, removing the earth in autumn endangers the trees during our severe winters; and 3d, it is not absolutely safe.

The best method, and I believe a cheaper than the above, is to dig them out in the fall, the last of September. The oozing gum leads to their quick detection, when they can be easily crushed. Our best pomologists, for fear some wee depredators escaped detection, go over the trees again in May.

This is not a tedious process, and should never be neglected. I have seen whole orchards languishing, and many trees killed outright by neglect to destroy these hateful miners. Such neglect in case of a fruit so rare, so delicious, and so profitable wherever it can be successfully grown, is unvenial.

Judge J. G. Ramsdell, so well and favorably known as a pomologist, tells me of a new method of mounding which is without the usual objections, and he claims a great saving of labor. He hooks tins around the trees,—the same used to keep the cut-worm at bay. These are some larger than the tree, and four or five inches wide. He fills in between them and the tree with earth. This is done about the first week of July, after the cut-worms have ceased work, and in time for the first eggs of the borer. In September he removes the tins and destroys the caterpillars, which can be done with far less labor than when we have to dig them from beneath the earth at its usual level.

Secretary Batcham of Ohio tells me that washing the base of the trees with the following compound is an effectual preventive, and he thinks the cheapest: Thin one quart of soft soap with water. Heat this to nearly the boiling temperature, then add one ounce carbolic acid in crystallized form. When cool, add ten times its bulk of water. Apply in July, with brush, to the base of the tree. This prevents egg-laying

---

PEAR OR CHERRY TREE SLUGS.

Selandria cerasi, Peck. Family, *Tenthredinidæ*. Sub-Order, *Hymenoptera*.

The destructive proclivities of these slimy "worms" are far too well known in our State. I have seen cherry trees in various localities badly injured by them, and the pear trees of one of our first pomologists almost destroyed. Few insects are so easily overcome; so with knowledge, vigilance, and promptness we may expect to soon be rid of a grievous pest.

NATURAL HISTORY.

The shining black fly, less than one-fourth of an inch long, appears in early and late summer. The eggs are deposited on the under side of the leaves. The larvæ (Fig. 36) are brown, possess twenty feet, taper posteriorly, and are covered with a viscid, olive-colored slime,—hence the name slug. Not all so-called slugs among insect larvæ are characterized by this unctuous covering, but all the larvæ of this destructive family may be quickly determined by the excessive number of legs, as they never contain less than eighteen, and sometimes as many as twenty-two. No other insect larvæ have to exceed sixteen,—the number gen-

FIG. 36.

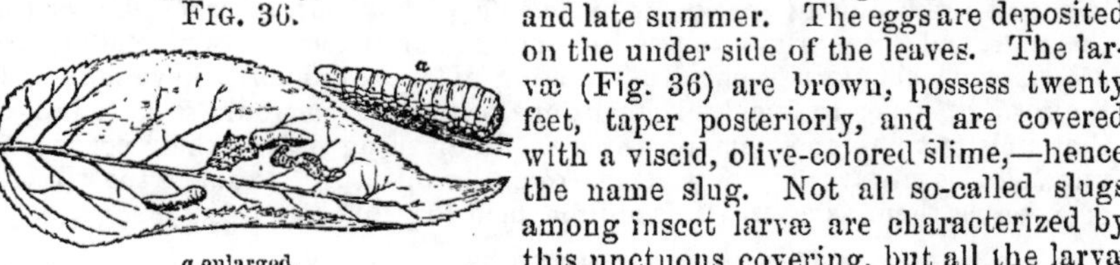

a enlarged.

erally possessed by caterpillars. These larvæ only eat the cuticle of the leaf, thus causing it to turn brown and sere. In three or four weeks the larvæ have matured, and pass down the tree and enter the earth, where they pupate, the flies of the first brood appearing late in August, those of the second late in May or early in June. These destructive insects belong to the very destructive family known as saw-flies, so named because of the wonderful organs terminating their bodies, which they use to form the groove for their eggs. As seen in the microscope, these organs are very beautiful, and would serve well for models of our instruments of the same name.

These cherry-tree slugs have been known to work on the plum tree, and some other of our shrubs.

REMEDIES.

The slime of these insects makes them peculiarly susceptible to any application like ashes, road dust (some deny that road dust is effectual), or lime. Hence, throwing any of the above substances into the tree where these insects are at work is sure to check their ravages. Such treatment goes to the root of the matter by destroying the source of the evil. These larvæ, as also those of other slugs, as the rose slug, so destructive in our State, and the pine tree slug, are destroyed by such solutions as white hellebore, quassia, Paris green with water, whale oil soap, carbolic acid, or coal oil. These last, of course, must be applied very weak, or the tree or plant will be injured. My friend, E. Reynolds, has killed the pine tree slug with Paris green, applied at my suggestion, one-half tablespoonful to a pail of water. The same remedy will banish the rose slug.

THE WEE PEACH BORER.

Tomicus liminaris, Harr. Family, *Scolytidæ*. Sub-Order, *Coleoptera*.

The summer immediately succeeding the hard winter of '72 and '73 I was called to the "Peach Belt" to examine a new peach borer, or at least a borer new to that region. I found, not a new enemy, but an old one in new quarters. Away back in Vol. IV., p. 502 of the American Horticulturist, I find Miss Morris describing this insect as working on the peach trees of the Middle States, and crediting it with causing the "yellows." It is quite propable that this insect will appear with the yellows, yet hardly I think as their cause: 1st, the insect appears where no yellows are found; 2d, the yellows show unmistakable evidence in many trees where none of these insects are found; and 3d, these insects work in some of our forest trees, which trees are diseased. Yet the unhealthy condition of the trees is far too great to be ascribed to the evils resulting from perhaps a quite limited number of insects. The conclusion, then, is, that these insects attack for the most part diseased trees, and thus trees with abated growth, or lessened vitality, from any reason, either yellows or severe cold, are specially liable to this farther injury, and we must needs take all the more pains to secure our orchards from injury.

NATURAL HISTORY.

This little beetle, less than one-tenth of an inch long, is of dark brown color. The wing cases are deeply furrowed, and abound with short hairs. This beetle so closely resembles a beetle that mines in the pine trees (*Tomicus pini*, Say), after doing immense damage, that the unscientific would hardly recognize them as distinct species. I found the beetles of both these insects during

July, but as these beetles looked very young, and as there were still many grubs even in the trees, I doubt not but the time as given by Harris, August, is nearer the average. I can not say where the eggs are laid,—perhaps on the bark,—yet, as we know of other insects of the same family that lay their eggs in the burrows, it is to be feared that this beetle has the same habits. The little whitish grubs eat all through the tree, so that some trees I saw were perfectly riddled with these minute tunnels, which were no larger than a common knitting-needle. The larvæ, pupæ, and imago may all be found in these tunnels during the first days of July. The beetles, prairie-dog like, appeared to be peering from their concealment; nor does the comparison end there, for upon the least disturbance they would beat a hasty retreat into their burrows.

REMEDIES.

I regret that I can offer no positive cure for this evil. As they burrow all through the trunk, we can not cut them out and burn them, as we could were they confined to branches. As their eggs are probably laid in the burrows, we are not sure that we can prohibit their being laid. Our only hope seems to be to render the trees obnoxious to the beetles during the months of July and August, when they issue from the trees.

I would use coal oil solution or carbolic acid solution, on the trunks, as the danger of injuring the trees would be slight. It may be found that common soap, or better, whale oil soap in strongest solution, will prevent the beetles from returning to the trees after mating. The peach orchardists along our western coasts must needs be on the alert for this enemy the coming season, for, as Mr. Bidwell well says, it is probable that our insect pests will be more than ever active this coming season, and will find our orchards illy prepared to resist their attacks. Let all try, who have occasion for their use, the several remedies recommended above, and report as to their efficacy.

PLANT LICE.

Aphis mali, Fabr., *A. cerrasi*, Fabr. Family, *Aphidæ*. Sub-Order, *Hemiptera*.

All our fruit men are familiar with the plant lice, as hardly a plant but suffers from the attack of some species. Yet, doubtless owing to the many natural enemies, and notwithstanding their wonderfully prolific tendencies, they are rarely very destructive. Sometimes they will attack a tree and seem to draw heavily upon its vitality, and the very next year not a single louse will be found on the tree. I have noticed this repeatedly.

NATURAL HISTORY.

These aphis, sometimes green, as is the case with the apple and rose aphis, and sometimes black, as seen in the species attacking the cherry, pass the winter as eggs. I speak of those left out of door. These hatch into females, which keep producing young, without any appearance of males, all summer through; so that the number of insects which may come from a single egg in a season is alarmingly prodigious. This may continue for eight or nine generations. But with the last brood in autumn there come forth true males and females. These pair and lay the eggs which are to produce the females in the succeeding spring. This kind of reproduction is not confined to plant lice. Other insects show the same peculiarity. In fact, it is a well demonstrated fact that drone bees are the product of unfertilized eggs. The two projecting tubes from the posterior parts of the flask-shaped bodies of these lice are called nectaries, as there exudes therefrom a sweet substance. This sweet secretion attracts the ants, hence the reason that we usually see plants attacked by lice also covered with ants. The lice and ants seem to dwell together very amicably. In fact, there seems to be an affection, not disinterested, to be sure, between them, as the ants caress the lice in a very loving manner, and in case of disturbance are very eager in their efforts to protect and care for the lice.

REMEDIES.

Syringing the plants with tobacco water is sure destruction to these insects. If limbs of small trees are alone attacked, they may be dipped in the fluid. Whale oil soap solution, and even common soap suds are beneficial, while many gardeners think that frequent syringing with pure water is not without benefit.

It has been recommended to brush the eggs off of young trees and small plants in the spring with a hand brush,—advice I think of doubtful practicality.

I think that these insects, where they are exposed to our cold winters and to the host of lice destroyers, will never do great mischief; but in our greenhouses and on our house plants they have full chance to work their ruin. But in these cases tobacco water and tobacco smoke are effectual preventives, and where else can this article, tobacco, be so appropriately used as in the destruction of these miserable lice?

IMPORTED CURRANT BORER.

Ægeria tipuliformis, Linn. Family, *Ægeridæ*. Sub-Order, *Lepidoptera*.

In an official communication lately received from App. M. Smith, secretary of the Manistee horticultural society, I am desired to give information in reference to the currant borer. Upon examination, I find that this insect is working its blighting ravages in this vicinity; so it is not unlikely that it is widely distributed throughout our State. This being the case, the reply to the Manistee pomologists will be of general interest.

As will be noticed, this beautiful wasp-like moth belongs to the same family and genus as the peach borer. The moths of this family may be readily told by their trim form, quick movements, diurnal habits, flying in the hot sunshine, and especially by the brush-like character of the tip of the body. This last character will serve to distinguish them from the wasps,—an important fact, as even entomologists of considerable experience are liable to be deceived, so striking is the resemblance. The larvæ of the family, so far as I know, are without exception borers. They are white with a brownish head, and generally pupate in a cocoon made of their own chips or dust.

This Ægerian, as will be noticed by the name, is imported, and, as is generally true, is all the worse from that fact. As a rule the imported species are the most destructive.

DESCRIPTION AND NATURAL HISTORY.

The moth is a little less than one-half inch long, and expands three-fourths of an inch. The color is deep blue, with three yellow bands across the abdomen, a yellow collar, and yellow mixed with blue marking the legs. These yellow bands, so like the same in many of our wasps, renders this species all the more liable to be mistaken, especially as they mingle with the wasps, making a gay company in the bright sunshine. Yet the tufted extremity, in lieu of a pointed one tipped with a dreaded spear, will quickly undeceive us.

These moths appear in June and July. I found several specimens yesterday, June 22. They deposit their eggs near a bud, at which work they seem very busily engaged during the heat of the day. These eggs soon hatch, and the tiny caterpillar at once bores to the center of the stem. What more strange than that this minute larva, almost microscopic, can thus perforate the hard, woody stem! These larvæ may be found in the stem from June to July the following year. I have taken the moth from the bushes with my net, and the nearly full-grown larvæ from the hollow stem the same day, June 22.

A curious example of wise foresight is afforded by these larvæ in their eating through the hard wood and bark before assuming the pupa state, as without such forecast and action the hollow stem would be a fatal dungeon to the moth, whose slender sucking tube and wanting jaws would render her escape hopeless.

In May, June, and July the insect becomes a pupa, the pupa always lying very near the outside opening, in a poor apology of a cocoon, if any, made of its own leavings. That able entomologist, Rev. C. J. S. Bethune of Ontario, speaks of the chrysalid sleeping peacefully in this cavity while the bleak wintry winds howl among the branches. (See Entomological Report of Ontario for the year 1871.) Such a remark would be true only of the larva.

In June and July the moths again appear.

These insects seem to attack the red currant more generally, yet the black variety, and even the gooseberry is not exempt from its blasting work. Not only do the broken stems, so weakened as to be unable to stand upright, but also the sickly appearance of the foliage tell of this insect's presence and work. Bending the stocks will also generally give the needed information, as the affected ones bend more readily. The hollows in stocks cut across will inform us of their previous or present work.

REMEDIES.

It has been suggested that we catch the moths. I think this is not a practical remedy. The moths are so small, so quick, so wasp-like, that I should despair of this ever becoming generally practiced. I would suggest letting the bushes sprout up pretty freely, and then each spring practice heavy pruning, taking pains to cut and burn the feeble and limber stocks. This should be done about May 20 ; if later, some of the earlier moths might escape, if earlier, the pruner could not discriminate so wisely between healthy and diseased stems

---

IMPORTED GOOSEBERRY SAW-FLY.

Nematus ventricosus, Klug. Family, *Tenthredinidæ*. Sub-Order, *Hymenoptera*.

This destructive insect, which has finally become scattered all over our State, is also a foreigner,—another of the many bequests from the old world which we would have gladly foregone. In view of the fact that we have received very many of our worst insect pests from Europe, they ought not to complain if we have given them *Phylloxera* or if we still add *Doryphora*, which they essay to prevent by laws prohibiting the importation of the potato. As well attempt to prevent the importation of rats by an interdict on the importation of seed packages. This gooseberry (or currant) slug is a fearful devastator, often completely defoliating the bushes the first year that it appears. Although only about fifteen years among us, still it is already broadly distributed throughout our State.

NATURAL HISTORY.

The yellow female saw-fly (Fig. 37, *b*), about the size of the house-fly, with black head, meets the smaller male (Fig. 37, *a*), which has more black, and commences laying her whitish transparent eggs along the veins underneath the leaf, about the first of May. These hatch in three or four days, and the green twenty-legged "worms" (Fig. 38, *a*), dotted with black until the last moult, when they are entirely green, commence immediately to feed on the leaves. These larvæ eat voraciously, and soon become full grown, being then three-fourths of an inch long. These larvæ either go into the earth, under leaves, or remain attached to the bushes and spin a cocoon of brownish silk. The larvæ will be found at work till in July. They remain as pupæ till the following spring, when the flies come forth to repeat the round of mischief.

FIG. 37.

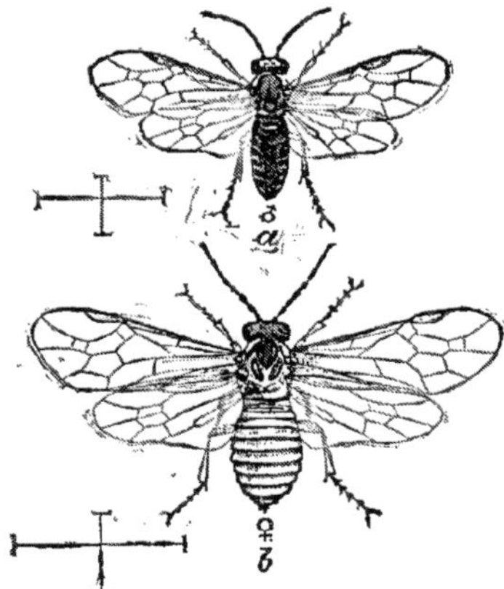

REMEDIES.

Prevention being universally conceded to be better than cure, all should be certain not to import these insects in procuring the plants. As the cocoons are hid in spring among the roots, these should be carefully washed and the material washed off burned. The absence of such precautionary measures accounts for the rapid spread of these pests.

The leaves when first worked on are perforated with small holes (Fig. 38). As there are comparatively few, the eggs being so compactly placed that but few leaves receive them, they can be gathered and burned. But if we have failed, either through ignorance or neglect, to destroy these destroyers till they become scattered over the bushes, we still can offer effectual battle. White hellebore, dusted upon the vine in the same manner that we would recommend for applying the Paris green mixture on the potato, is sure destruction to these "worms." This is best applied when there is little or no wind; and, though poisonous, is entirely safe if used cautiously. If it is preferred, as in most cases it doubtless will be, the hellebore may be mixed with water and applied with a sprinkler, in which case we are independent of wind and can not inhale it. An ounce to a pail of water is sufficient. As it costs but forty cents per pound, it will be seen that it is not expensive.*

FIG. 38.

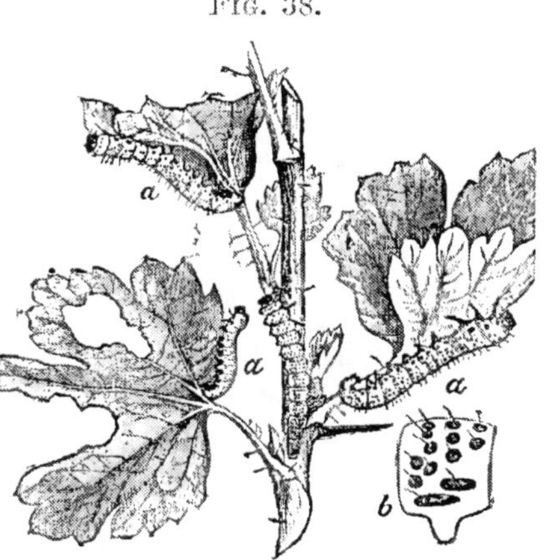

The fruit will receive so slight an amount of the hellebore that no fear need be entertained in using it,—in fact the first rain will wash it off,—and if any are afraid, they can easily rinse the fruit before using it. It has long been used in Europe, and no harm is reported.

Elder Potter of Lansing states that dusting the bushes with ashes kills the insects, while Wm. M. Clark of the same city gives like evidence as to soap-suds. Still, neither of these can take the place of the hellebore, which, if a good article, will prove effective every time, by whomsoever used; which is not the case with either of the other substances.

THE CURRANT MEASURING WORM.

Abraxis ribearia, Fitch. Family, *Phalænidæ*. Sub-Order, *Lepidoptera*.

This insect has caused so little damage in our State that until last year I have never heard of it as doing injury among us. Last season I received the moths from several localities, in some of which the larvæ did considerable damage. I have taken the moth at Lansing for several years, and have seen the larvæ working on the wild bushes, gooseberry and currant, but have never met it in our gardens.

NATURAL HISTORY.

This species exist during the winter as eggs. Late in May the larvæ appear, which are white, striped with yellow, and dotted with black (Fig. 39), and can easily be told by the same peculiarity noted in the canker worm,—the habit of measuring (1, Fig. 39), or looping, when they move, and dropping (2, Fig. 39) by a thread when disturbed. By the last of June they are full grown, and measure a little more than an inch in length. The larvæ pass into the earth to pupate, and a little beneath the surface change to a brown chrysalis about one-half of an inch long (3, Fig. 39). In about two weeks the moths appear. These are of a pale yellowish color, with more or less dusky spots on the wings, which frequently form a band across the wings. Sometimes the dusky spots are slight. The moths (Fig 40), expand 1¼ inches. The moths lay their eggs along the twigs, where they remain, despite the heat and cold, till another spring.

FIG. 39.

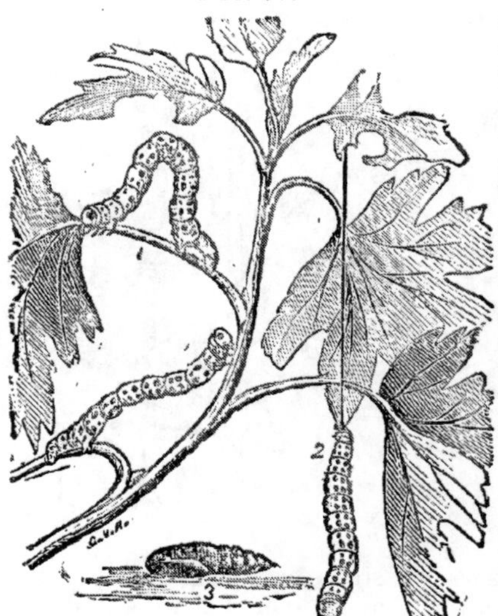

REMEDIES.

The moths can be caught in a net; and though this is easily done, still it is not as practical a remedy as the hellebore, which by many is reported to be as efficient as with the saw-fly larvæ. As it was reported a failure during the past season by several persons, I can but think that the hellebore was not the genuine article, or else was very poor.

Hand-picking is more than usually easy of adoption, to be practiced in the same manner as with the canker worms: give the bush a slight tap, when the larvæ will drop, and remain suspended by a thread for some time. By using a stick these can be drawn out together and easily crushed.

FIG. 40.

It is more than likely that this pest, which has been long destructive east, will continue to be more and more so with us as our forests are cut away, removing its native foliage. Let us all give it battle from the outset.

CLIMBING CUT-WORMS.

Agrotis Cochrani. Riley.

Were the climbing cut-worms as destructive in all sections of our State as they are along our eastern and western shores, these insects would rank next to the Codling Moth as a pest of the orchardist, and even now they occupy no inferior position. It would be difficult to estimate the amount of damage which these insects have perpetrated in our State. They not only strip the buds from our fruit trees, but the various vines also minister to their appetites.

NATURAL HISTORY.

Little need be said on this subject farther than what has been said in reference to field cut-worms, as the characters of the various cut-worms are very similar, as also their habits; yet, just before the larvæ matures, the climbing species exhibit a strange peculiarity, as during the warm summer nights they come forth from their earthen retreats, not to nip the tender corn or tomato plant, but to climb some apple, pear, or peach tree, or some grape vine, and eat out the tender buds, thus frequently doing irreparable damage. The owner sees the damage, but not the enemy, and all ignorant of the true cause, says hard things of his bird friends. These have wrought great injury at Monroe the past season, yet hardly a sufferer knew the cause of the mischief. These larvæ hide by day just beneath the ground, where they may be found by a little digging. They may also be seen by climbing into the trees by night or by shaking the same, when the "worms" will fall to the earth. There are two or three species in our State that I am sure have this climbing habit; there may be several.

REMEDIES.

In addition to the process of digging out by hand, recommended to destroy field cut-worms, and placing armfulls of fresh clover to entrap the larvæ, as already suggested to the gardener, there are still other methods to fight or ward off the climbing species. They can be caught by using the sheet and mallet at night, as in fighting the curculio when they are in the tree. They may also be kept from gaining access to the tree or vines at all. To protect vines Prof. Tracy recommends using stiff smooth paper, about four inches wide. He winds this about the trunk, gathering in at the top, and tying about this gathered portion with a cord, drawing it tightly. The lower portion is permitted to stand out a little from the tree, so the whole resembles an inverted funnel. For larger trees, and indeed for small trees and vines, the same is often used, but tin bands will be most desirable. The tin should be thin and bright, and should be cut into strips about three inches wide, and of a length to correspond to the size of the trees to be protected. When these are drawn closely about the tree they should lap sufficiently to be tacked or nailed through the lap: a hole should be made through one end of the tins with a punch, then in placing the tins on the tree the end with the hole should lap over the other end, and if a lath nail is used this may be made by a smart blow to pass through the other end, and into the tree. The nail should only be driven partially in so as to be easily pulled out when the tins are to be laid away. By making a narrow slit in the other end of the tin to correspond with the hole when the tin is lapped, it can be fastened by a common carpet tack, in which case the tack should only be driven partially in to the tree. Prof. Tracy recommends that the tin be tacked or nailed near the upper edge. This tin is a sure preventive, for the cut-worm cannot pass over the surface of smooth tin. Judge Ramsdell would have the tins longer, and fasten by hooking, as the ends are bent for that purpose. He thinks there is little danger of the larva passing between the band and tree. He uses these same bands in fighting the peach borer, as already described.

As these pests work far worse on sandy land, those having orchards on light soil will have to be specially vigilant.

Had this remedy been known and practiced, how much would have been saved to our State! Now that it is known, shall we not all practice, and stop this leak in our treasury?

THE ROSE CHAFER.

Macrodactylus subspinosa, Fabr. Family, *Scarabeidæ*. Sub-Order, *Coleoptera*.

As this old pest of the rose is becoming quite destructive to the grape in various sections of our State, it demands a brief notice.

NATURAL HISTORY.

Its history and habits closely resemble those of its family relation, the May beetle, already described.

FIG. 41.

The beetles (Fig. 41) appear in June and July; eat most ravenously, seeming to relish rose leaves, grape leaves, and even cherry leaves. After this wedding feast is over, the females lay their eggs in the ground. The grubs feed on the roots of plants, but are not sufficiently destructive to attract attention. The pupæ may be found in May, and in June the beetles come forth again to their work of plunder.

REMEDIES.

As this beetle will, like the curculio and blister beetles, fall from the plants whenever disturbed, they may be shaken on to sheets placed under the vines, and destroyed.

I presume that white hellebore might destroy these beetles, and there is hardly any doubt but that they would succumb to Paris green, which I think would be perfectly safe when applied so early in the season. As we have none of these beetles here, I can not experiment with these various remedies. Let some of our fruit men along the lake shore try these applications, as also that of a solution of carbolic acid, not strong enough to injure the vines, and report the results.

GRAPE-VINE LEAF-HOPPER.

Erythroneura vitis, Harr. Family, *Cicadellina*. Sub-Order, *Hemiptera*.

These sprightly little insects are quite generally distributed through our State, and though they are specially ruinous some seasons, yet perhaps the very next they are not to be met at all. I think Mr. Bidwell of South Haven has discovered the cause of this sudden disappearance, and in it a method to successfully fight them.

NATURAL HISTORY.

These beautiful little insects (Fig. 42), so gaily robed in yellow, black, and scarlet, hybernate during the winter in the mature state, and may be found in fall and winter just under the vines, protected from the fatal damp by the leaves. In the spring the survivors come forth, lay their eggs on the plants, and soon die. The young are quite like the parents, except in size and absence of wings. They possess the same hopping propensity, and hence the lively appearance whenever the vines are disturbed. The insects continue to grow, become possessed of wings, and if very abundant will well nigh suck the vitality all out of the vines.

FIG. 42.

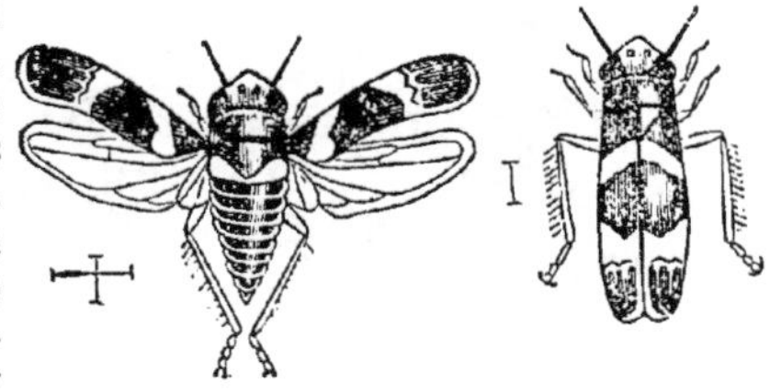

REMEDIES.

Mr. Bidwell discovered, in collecting these hoppers one winter, that those which were under damp leaves were dead, and only those which were protected from the damp of winter survived. Hence the only practical remedy I have ever heard of for these pests of our vineyards: As soon as they have become dormant in winter, so rake up the leaves under the vines as to cause the insects to become a prey to this inability to endure wet or damp. I think it would be well to rake up the leaves in autumn and burn them, doing it on cold days, when the hoppers are dormant, and before the vines are laid down for winter.

THE GRAPE PHYLLOXERA.

Phylloxera vastatrix, Plan. Family, *Aphidae*. Sub-order, *Hemiptera*.

This little insect, hardly large enough to attract the attention of any but the cautious observer, is without doubt an American insect. Yet, from the comparative immunity of most of the grapes grown here from its blighting attacks, and ignorance of its natural history, only a part of such history being known, it was not dreamed, when Prof. Planchon announced, in 1868, that the cause of the terrible Phylloxera plague of France was a minute plant louse, that the insect was identical with that described as *Phylloxera vitifoliæ* by Dr. Fitch, twelve years before. At last the assurance seems to be conclusive that the insects are identical, though some still believe otherwise, yet with no sufficient reason, I think, and that we have suffered more or less during all our grape-growing history from the ravages of this insect, whose late importation is striking far more serious blows at this important interest in Europe.

NATURAL HISTORY.

The dull orange colored louse described by Dr. Fitch, which by puncturing the leaves causes them to become covered with excrescences or small galls (Fig. 43) which greatly deform the leaf, are but one form of this insect, and that by far the most harmless.

FIG. 43.

Under side of leaf, showing galls.

Under these galls the eggs (Fig. 44, *d*) are laid to the number of three or four hundred. These soon hatch, and the young lice (Fig 44, *a*, *b*) go merrily forth in their bright yellow garb, and repeat the work of their parents. Thus on, for four or five generations, all the lice are wingless, all females,—in fact, no other ever appear in the galls. What is very curious, only a few varieties suffer from these not very serious leaf galls, the Clinton seeming to be most susceptible to such attacks. As fall approaches the galls become deserted, and the young descend to the roots, where they hibernate. As these gall lice will readily take to the roots and flourish if removed to those vines where the galls are never found, it is not improbable that some lice pass from leaves to roots during the summer. Why some of the lice pass to the leaves of certain varieties of grapes in the summer is yet unknown. It may be possible that they prefer roots when they are suitable, and will only attack leaves when the roots are not to their taste, which may be true of the Clinton. This is certainly a reasonable conjecture, if the edible character of the grape is any index to that of the root.

FIG. 44.

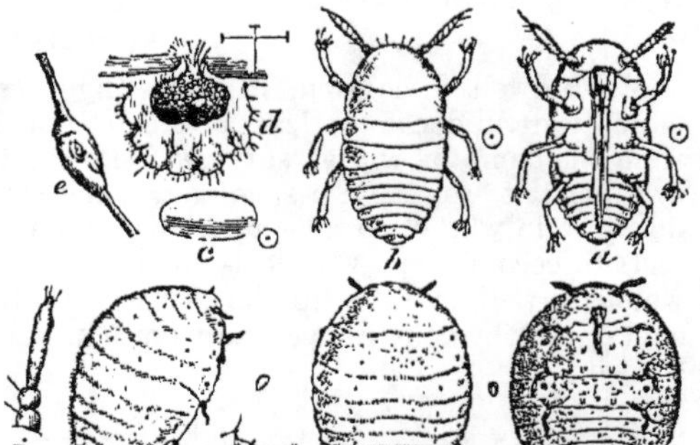

a and *b*, larvæ as seen from below and above; *c*, egg; *d*, gall; *e* enlarged tendrils; *f*, *g*, and *h*, imago gall, louse from side, above, and below; *i*, antennæ; *j* tarsus—side marks show true size.

Unfortunately there is another form of this louse,—the root form, for it is this form which has given to the future of grape growing in Europe its uncertainty. The young (Fig. 45, *b*) of this form are not distinguishable from those of the galls. Not so with the more mature forms (Fig. 45, *e*, *f*, *g*), which are not smooth, like those formed in the galls, but are covered with warts. Some of these assume a greenish cast, become large before and taper back, and, like the gall-forms, are always without wings. The others are always bright yellow, always of the oval form of the young, and finally develop stubs of wings (Fig. 47, *e*, *f*), and at last come forth with well-developed wings (Fig. 47, *g*, *h*), well equipped to go forth to new fields for conquest. They come forth from the earth as pupa, and then cast their skin for the last

Fig. 45.

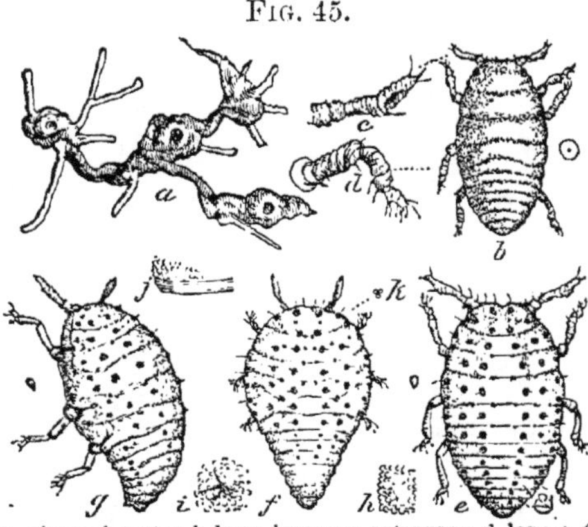

a, diseased roots; *b*, larva louse; *c*, antennae; *d*, leg; *e*, *f*, and *g*, imago root lice; *h*, granulations on the skin; *i*, tubercle.

time. These winged forms are still yellow, but have lost their tubercles. The winged forms are most abundant in August and September, though they may be seen from July till fall. The most of these are long, lay eggs, and are certainly females. Others are shorter of body, and are supposed by some to be males, but are probably abortive females. These lay eggs from which come the true male (Fig. 46) and female, which latter lays but a single egg. These all die off in fall, so that the insects pass the winter either as eggs or as larvæ.

This polymorphism, or different forms of the same species, is not peculiar to lice, but is shown in even the highest insects, as seen in the bees and ants.

Fig. 46.

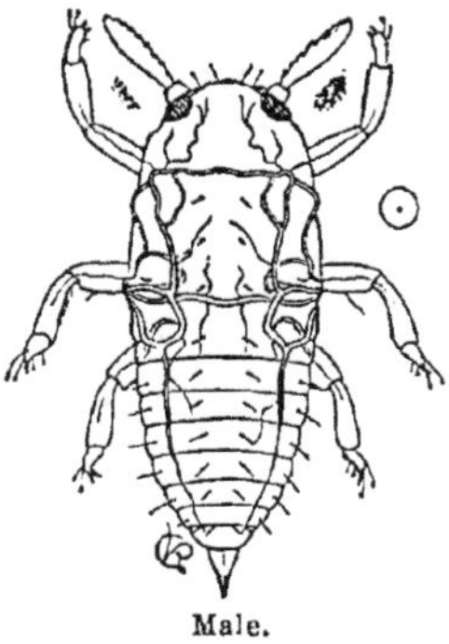

Male.

As already intimated, some entomologists deny the identity of these forms, especially the gall and root form. Now, as it is not exceptional among insects, and as Prof. Riley, who has done himself great credit by his thorough and skillful investigations of this insect, has produced the gall form from the young of the root form, and *vice versa*, it seems to me that doubt should be entirely banished. Besides, any vineyard, so far as I have examined, which has in it both Clinton and Catawba grape vines, will have both these forms if either.

The roots which are attacked by these lice, swell, become deformed (Fig. 47, *d*), and in three or four years rot. The first season the vines above ground show no signs of the evil; the second they become yellow and sickly, and frequently die the third season.

HOW THE INSECTS SPREAD.

The wingless root forms pass from the roots of one vine to those of another, and thus spread the disease. Very likely the young from the galls are blown from one vine to another, as we know the young of the oyster-shell bark-lice are. The winged females may fly, by aid of the wind, to an indefinite distance, and as a single female may become the parent of millions of lice in a single season, we can easily see why all Europe is in alarm.

VARIETIES OF GRAPES SUSCEPTIBLE TO THE ROOT FORM.

Of the grapes grown and recommended for cultivation in this State, fortunately very few are subject to serious harm from the root form of the Phylloxera, the only form that does serious damage. The vigorous, rapid-growing varieties are almost exempt, while the slow growers are very apt to suffer. The Concord, Hartford Prolific, and Israella are almost entirely exempt, as is the Clinton. The Delaware, Crevelling, Rebecca, Diana, Eumelan, and Allen's

Fig. 47.

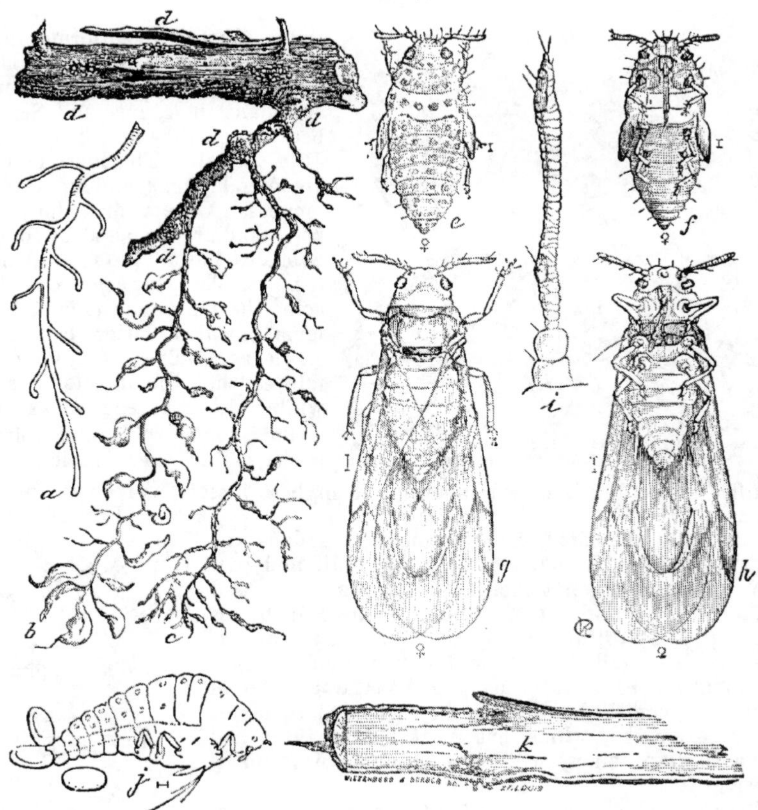

a, healthy root; *b*, root on which the lice are at work; *c*, deserted root where decay has commenced; *d*, lice on large roots; *e* and *f*, pupæ; *g* and *h*, imagos with wings; *i*, antennæ of same; *j*, wingless female on roots depositing; *k*, section of root.

Hybrid are more susceptible, but comparatively undisturbed; while the Iona and Catawba are very liable to attack and injury. Who knows how much the want of success with the Catawba and Iona is consequent upon the ravages of the Phylloxera. I have seen the injurious effects of this pest at Pointe aux Peaux, Monroe county, and more marked still in the famous vineyards of Kelley's Island, Ohio.

Fortunately there are a host of natural enemies which, especially in this country, will go very far towards holding the pest in abeyance.

PREVENTIVES.

Grafting the susceptible varieties on such stocks as the Clinton, Concord, or Israella has been recommended, and is being extensively tried, especially in Europe. Mr. Kelley of Kelley's Island, who has experimented some, has little faith in grafting; yet my observations at his place were encouraging.* In procuring vines, it would be a safe precaution to dip the roots in some insecticide,

* Prof. Riley, who has just returned from Europe, tells me that the grafting experiments tried there grafting their varieties on our stocks is giving great hope as an effectual cure for this terrible plague.

as a strong solution of whale-oil soap, before setting them. It would be well, too, to mix soot in the soil, as that is found obnoxious to the lice.

DIRECT REMEDIES.

The leaves affected with galls should be collected and destroyed early in the season. Submersion for twenty or thirty days has been found effectual in France in killing the root forms. Wherever this can be done it should be brought into requisition in autumn, immediately after the season's growth is complete. It is said that at this season the vines will not suffer, even if submerged for a time sufficient to destroy the lice.

Carbolic acid powder and soot are highly recommended. By mixing these with the soil the lice are said to be destroyed.

Bisulphide of carbon, which we use so successfully in destroying museum pests, which recently gave so much hope in France, is now given up as too expensive, too laborious of application, and not thorough enough in its effects, owing, doubtless, to inability to reach the lice in making the application.

According to late advices Prof. Dumas, of the French academy, has discovered a perfect remedy, and one easily applied. It is the salt: potassic sulphocarbonate (K S C S^2), which is applied in a dry form. It is placed on the earth beneath the vines and carried to the roots by the rain. The efficacy of this salt is vouched for by such well known scientists as Messrs. Milne Edwards, Posteur, Duchartre, Blanchard, etc. As I have before suggested, our ability is ever commensurate with our needs.

CLOTHES MOTH.

Tinea flavi-frontella, Linn. Family, *Tineidæ*. Sub-order *Lepidoptera*.

Hon. W. L. Webber of East Saginaw writes: "We of this place (East Saginaw) are very much troubled with carpet and furniture moths. If your time would permit, I think a paper prepared by you, giving the details of the natural history, habits, and transformations of this pest, and the best method to prevent its work or to get rid of it after work has commenced, will be of great interest to us here, and I believe of general interest."

I take pleasure in complying with the above request, not simply because of the importance of the subject, but also because of the general ignorance in regard to it, even among those most cultured and most interested. Only a few evenings since, when I was taking tea with one of the best informed ladies of my acquaintance, I called her attention to some of the pretty little yellow moths just coming from her elegant furniture. "What!" she remarked, "those the moths! I supposed the large ones [cut-worm moths, *Agrotians*] we see behind the blinds in summer and autumn were the mischief-makers." It would be no greater mistake to call an elephant a horse.

DESCRIPTION.

These little moths expand about a half inch, and are less than one-fourth of an inch long. They are of a light buff color, and shine like satin. The wings are long, narrow, pointed, and beautifully fringed. The larva ("worm") is white, with a yellow head, has, like nearly all caterpillars, sixteen legs, and is always surrounded by a flattened, cylindrical case, usually gray or whitish in color, though this depends on their food. The ends are open, that the larvæ may reach forth to feed, or peer forth, which they are free to do when disturbed.

The pupa or chrysalis is somewhat curved, and has a rounded head. The antennæ, wings, and legs are folded beneath the body, and reach nearly to the end of the body. The pupa case or cocoon is similar to the larva case.

HABITS.

The moth comes forth as early as the last of May, and may be seen from that time till the close of summer. Their tiny, lustrous, buff-colored bodies are easily detected, as they rest with wings folded close about their bodies in the deep crevices of our parlor furniture, or among the folds of our garments, or even more plainly as they flit across our rooms.

These moths pair, after which the female seeks out our furs and woolen or silk apparel, her minute size enabling her to enter drawers, closets, and trunks; when she distributes her eggs with an eye to the good of her prospective young, if not to our good. The larvæ soon appear, and may be found at home the summer through, comfortably fixed up in their little tents and working their miserable mischief, all unsuspected by the unwary housewife, who learns too late of their previous presence, by discovering that her most choice possessions are totally ruined. In spring and summer the chrysalids will appear, soon to followed by a new return of the pretty moths.

REMEDIES.

Woolen garments and furs should be put away in trunks, with several pieces of camphor gum as large as hickory-nuts packed in with them, or they may be put in close paper bags and pasted up so that no holes, ever so small, will remain open. Even in this case a little camphor gum will render assurance doubly sure. Infested garments or furs should be put in a tight sack or trunk, and after adding a half ounce of chloroform the sack or trunk should be closed as nearly air tight as possible. The vapor will kill the insects. Then prepare as given above.

For furniture and carpets heavy paper, wet with carbolic acid or spirits of turpentine, will kill larvæ already at work. This should be placed under the edge of the carpet, where the mischief is generally done, and in furniture, crowded back in the deep folds. It would be well to saturate the interior of the furniture with a strong solution of carbolic acid. Our best furniture and furs have a goodly quantity of this substance in the undissolved state fastened inside them when made. Russian leather, cedar bark or boughs, tobacco leaves, and even red pepper, are said to prevent the moths from laying eggs. It will be well, then, to place these in exposed situations. Manufacturers of carriages wash the woolen linings of their carriages with a weak solution of corrosive sublimate, which is very sure destruction to all insects. Yet Dr. Kedzie tells me it is unsafe to use it.

Hon. W. L. Webber writes me as follows in reference to a method practiced by his people in destroying the larvæ in carpets:

"There is one means which they have practiced of killing the worm while in the carpet which is not suggested by your article. Take a wet sheet or other cloth, lay it upon the carpet, and then run a hot flat-iron over it, so as to convert the water into steam, which permeates the carpet beneath and destroys the life of the inchoate moth. They have found this very successful, and as it can be done without taking up the carpet, and the whole surface gone over in a comparatively short time, it is regarded as one of the most efficient means of protection they have."

Every careful housekeeper will carefully examine her carpets and furniture each fall and spring, brush out all the creases, give all a good airing, and if there is any trace of these evil-doers, will practice the above remedies.

A. J. COOK,

LANSING, June 10, 1875. *Professor in Agricultural College.*

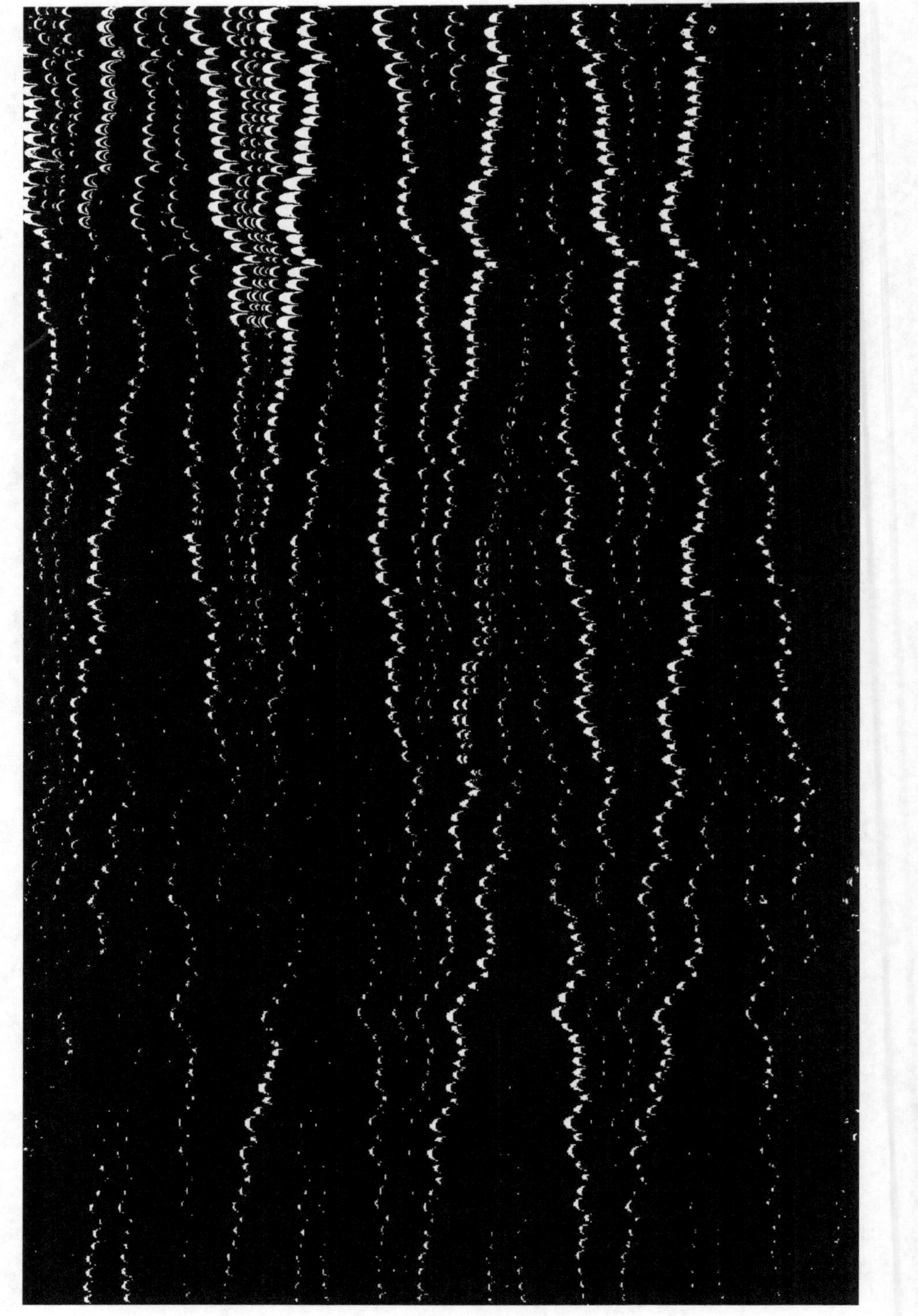

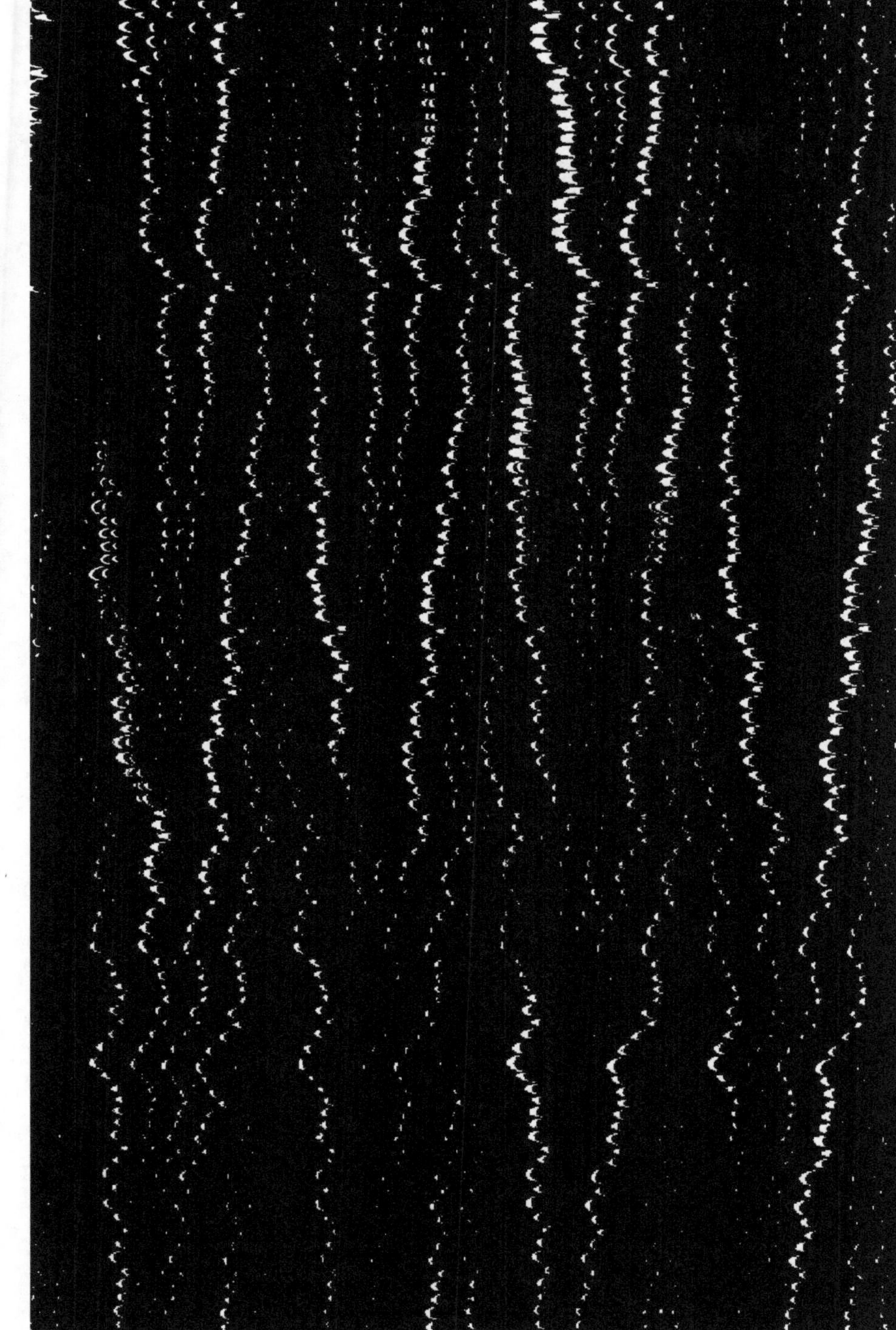

Printed in the USA
CPSIA information can be obtained
at www.ICGtesting.com
LVHW012122070824
787627LV00007B/311